CASENOTE® Legal Briefs ®

PROFESSIONAL RESPONSIBILITY

Keyed to Courses Using

**Gillers's
Regulation of Lawyers:
Problems of Law and Ethics
Eleventh Edition**

Authored by: Publisher's Editorial Staff

. Wolters Kluwer

Copyright © 2018 CCH Incorporated. All Rights Reserved.

Published by Wolters Kluwer in New York.

Wolters Kluwer Legal & Regulatory U.S. serves customers worldwide with CCH, Aspen Publishers, and Kluwer Law International products. (www.WKLegaledu.com)

No part of this publication may be reproduced or transmitted in any form or by any means, electronic or mechanical, including photocopy, recording, or utilized by any information storage and retrieval system, without written permission from the publisher. For information about permissions or to request permissions online, visit us at www.WKLegaledu.com, or a written request may be faxed to our permissions department at 212-771-0803.

To contact Customer Service, e-mail customer.service@wolterskluwer.com, call 1-800-234-1660, fax 1-800-901-9075, or mail correspondence to:

Wolters Kluwer
Attn: Order Department
P.O. Box 990
Frederick, MD 21705

Printed in the United States of America.

1 2 3 4 5 6 7 8 9 0

ISBN 978-1-4548-9861-0

About Wolters Kluwer Legal & Regulatory U.S.

Wolters Kluwer Legal & Regulatory U.S. delivers expert content and solutions in the areas of law, corporate compliance, health compliance, reimbursement, and legal education. Its practical solutions help customers successfully navigate the demands of a changing environment to drive their daily activities, enhance decision quality and inspire confident outcomes.

Serving customers worldwide, its legal and regulatory portfolio includes products under the Aspen Publishers, CCH Incorporated, Kluwer Law International, ftwilliam.com and MediRegs names. They are regarded as exceptional and trusted resources for general legal and practice-specific knowledge, compliance and risk management, dynamic workflow solutions, and expert commentary.

Format for the Casenote® Legal Brief

Nature of Case: This section identifies the form of action (e.g., breach of contract, negligence, battery), the type of proceeding (e.g., demurrer, appeal from trial court's jury instructions), or the relief sought (e.g., damages, injunction, criminal sanctions).

Palsgraf v. Long Island R.R. Co.

Injured bystander (P) v. Railroad company (D)

N.Y. Ct. App., 248 N.Y. 339, 162 N.E. 99 (1928).

Party ID: Quick identification of the relationship between the parties.

Fact Summary: This is included to refresh your memory and can be used as a quick reminder of the facts.

NATURE OF CASE: Appeal from judgment affirming verdict for plaintiff seeking damages for personal injury.

FACT SUMMARY: Helen Palsgraf (P) was injured on R.R.'s (D) train platform when R.R.'s (D) guard helped a passenger aboard a moving train, causing his package to fall on the tracks. The package contained fireworks which exploded, creating a shock that tipped a scale onto Palsgraf (P).

though unintended, could have been averted or avoided by observance of such a duty. The scope of the duty is limited by the range of danger that a reasonable person could foresee. In this case, there was nothing to suggest from the appearance of the parcel or otherwise that the parcel contained fireworks. The guard could not reasonably have had any warning of a threat to Palsgraf (P), and R.R. (D) therefore cannot be held liable. Judgment is reversed in favor of R.R. (D).

Rule of Law: Summarizes the general principle of law that the case illustrates. It may be used for instant recall of the court's holding and for classroom discussion or home review.

🏛 RULE OF LAW
The risk reasonably to be perceived defines the duty to be obeyed.

FACTS: Helen Palsgraf (P) purchased a ticket to Rockaway Beach from R.R. (D) and was waiting on the train platform. As she waited, two men ran to catch a train that was pulling out from the platform. The first man jumped aboard, but the second man, who appeared as if he might fall, was helped aboard by the guard on the train who had kept the door open so they could jump aboard. A guard on the platform also helped by pushing him onto the train. The man was carrying a package wrapped in newspaper. In the process, the man dropped his package, which fell on the tracks. The package contained fireworks and exploded. The shock of the explosion was apparently of great enough strength to tip over some scales at the other end of the platform, which fell on Palsgraf (P) and injured her. A jury awarded her damages, and R.R. (D) appealed.

ISSUE: Does the risk reasonably to be perceived define the duty to be obeyed?

HOLDING AND DECISION: (Cardozo, C.J.) Yes. The risk reasonably to be perceived defines the duty to be obeyed. If there is no foreseeable hazard to the injured party as the result of a seemingly innocent act, the act does not become a tort because it happened to be a wrong as to another. If the wrong was not willful, the plaintiff must show that the act as to her had such great and apparent possibilities of danger as to entitle her to protection. Negligence in the abstract is not enough upon which to base liability. Negligence is a relative concept, evolving out of the common law doctrine of trespass on the case. To establish liability, the defendant must owe a legal duty of reasonable care to the injured party. A cause of action in tort will lie where harm,

DISSENT: (Andrews, J.) The concept that there is no negligence unless R.R. (D) owes a legal duty to take care as to Palsgraf (P) herself is too narrow. Everyone owes to the world at large the duty of refraining from those acts that may unreasonably threaten the safety of others. If the guard's action was negligent as to those nearby, it was also negligent as to those outside what might be termed the "danger zone." For Palsgraf (P) to recover, R.R.'s (D) negligence must have been the proximate cause of her injury, a question of fact for the jury.

Concurrence/Dissent: All concurrences and dissents are briefed whenever they are included by the casebook editor.

▶ ANALYSIS
The majority defined the limit of the defendant's liability in terms of the danger that a reasonable person in defendant's situation would have perceived. The dissent argued that the limitation should not be placed on liability, but rather on damages. Judge Andrews suggested that only injuries that would not have happened but for R.R.'s (D) negligence should be compensable. Both the majority and dissent recognized the policy-driven need to limit liability for negligent acts, seeking, in the words of Judge Andrews, to define a framework "that will be practical and in keeping with the general understanding of mankind." The Restatement (Second) of Torts has accepted Judge Cardozo's view.

Analysis: This last paragraph gives you a broad understanding of where the case "fits in" with other cases in the section of the book and with the entire course. It is a hornbook-style discussion indicating whether the case is a majority or minority opinion and comparing the principal case with other cases in the casebook. It may also provide analysis from restatements, uniform codes, and law review articles. The analysis will prove to be invaluable to classroom discussion.

Quicknotes

FORESEEABILITY A reasonable expectation that change is the probable result of certain acts or omissions.

NEGLIGENCE Conduct falling below the standard of care that a reasonable person would demonstrate under similar conditions.

PROXIMATE CAUSE The natural sequence of events without which an injury would not have been sustained.

Fact Summary: This is included to refresh your memory and can be used as a quick reminder of the facts.

Rule of Law: Summarizes the general principle of law that the case illustrates. It may be used for instant recall of the court's holding and for classroom discussion or home review.

Facts: This section contains all relevant facts of the case, including the contentions of the parties and the lower court holdings. It is written in a logical order to give the student a clear understanding of the case. The plaintiff and defendant are identified by their proper names throughout and are always labeled with a (P) or (D).

Issue: The issue is a concise question that brings out the essence of the opinion as it relates to the section of the casebook in which the case appears. Both substantive and procedural issues are included if relevant to the decision.

Holding and Decision: This section offers a clear and in-depth discussion of the rule of the case and the court's rationale. It is written in easy-to-understand language and answers the issue presented by applying the law to the facts of the case. When relevant, it includes a thorough discussion of the exceptions to the case as listed by the court, any major cites to the other cases on point, and the names of the judges who wrote the decisions.

Quicknotes: Conveniently defines legal terms found in the case and summarizes the nature of any statutes, codes, or rules referred to in the text.

Wolters Kluwer Legal & Regulatory U.S. is proud to offer *Casenote® Legal Briefs*—continuing thirty years of publishing America's best-selling legal briefs.

Casenote® Legal Briefs are designed to help you save time when briefing assigned cases. Organized under convenient headings, they show you how to abstract the basic facts and holdings from the text of the actual opinions handed down by the courts. Used as part of a rigorous study regimen, they can help you spend more time analyzing and critiquing points of law than on copying bits and pieces of judicial opinions into your notebook or outline.

Casenote® Legal Briefs should never be used as a substitute for assigned casebook readings. They work best when read as a follow-up to reviewing the underlying opinions themselves. Students who try to avoid reading and digesting the judicial opinions in their casebooks or online sources will end up shortchanging themselves in the long run. The ability to absorb, critique, and restate the dynamic and complex elements of case law decisions is crucial to your success in law school and beyond. It cannot be developed vicariously.

Casenote® Legal Briefs represents but one of the many offerings in Legal Education's Study Aid Timeline, which includes:

- *Casenote® Legal Briefs*
- *Emanuel® Law Outlines*
- Emanuel® *Law in a Flash* Flash Cards
- Emanuel® *CrunchTime®* Series

Each of these series is designed to provide you with easy-to-understand explanations of complex points of law. Each volume offers guidance on the principles of legal analysis and, consulted regularly, will hone your ability to spot relevant issues. We have titles that will help you prepare for class, prepare for your exams, and enhance your general comprehension of the law along the way.

To find out more about our law school tools for success, visit us at *www.WKLegaledu.com* or email us at *legaledu@wolterskluwer.com*. We'll be happy to assist you.

A. Decide on a Format and Stick to It

Structure is essential to a good brief. It enables you to arrange systematically the related parts that are scattered throughout most cases, thus making manageable and understandable what might otherwise seem to be an endless and unfathomable sea of information. There are, of course, an unlimited number of formats that can be utilized. However, it is best to find one that suits your needs and stick to it. Consistency breeds both efficiency and the security that when called upon you will know where to look in your brief for the information you are asked to give.

Any format, as long as it presents the essential elements of a case in an organized fashion, can be used. Experience, however, has led *Casenote*® *Legal Briefs* to develop and utilize the following format because of its logical flow and universal applicability.

NATURE OF CASE: This is a brief statement of the legal character and procedural status of the case (e.g., "Appeal of a burglary conviction").

There are many different alternatives open to a litigant dissatisfied with a court ruling. The key to determining which one has been used is to discover *who is asking this court for what*.

This first entry in the brief should be kept as *short as possible*. Use the court's terminology if you understand it. But since jurisdictions vary as to the titles of pleadings, the best entry is the one that addresses who wants what in this proceeding, not the one that sounds most like the court's language.

RULE OF LAW: A statement of the general principle of law that the case illustrates (e.g., "An acceptance that varies any term of the offer is considered a rejection and counteroffer").

Determining the rule of law of a case is a procedure similar to determining the issue of the case. Avoid being fooled by red herrings; there may be a few rules of law mentioned in the case excerpt, but usually only one is *the* rule with which the casebook editor is concerned. The techniques used to locate the issue, described below, may also be utilized to find the rule of law. Generally, your best guide is simply the chapter heading. It is a clue to the point the casebook editor seeks to make and should be kept in mind when reading every case in the respective section.

FACTS: A synopsis of only the essential facts of the case, i.e., those bearing upon or leading up to the issue.

The facts entry should be a short statement of the events and transactions that led one party to initiate legal proceedings against another in the first place. While some cases conveniently state the salient facts at the beginning of the decision, in other instances they will have to be culled from hiding places throughout the text, even from concurring and dissenting opinions. Some of the "facts" will often be in dispute and should be so noted. Conflicting evidence may be briefly pointed up. "Hard" facts must be included. Both must be *relevant* in order to be listed in the facts entry. It is impossible to tell what is relevant until the entire case is read, as the ultimate determination of the rights and liabilities of the parties may turn on something buried deep in the opinion.

Generally, the facts entry should not be longer than three to five *short* sentences.

It is often helpful to identify the role played by a party in a given context. For example, in a construction contract case the identification of a party as the "contractor" or "builder" alleviates the need to tell that that party was the one who was supposed to have built the house.

It is always helpful, and a good general practice, to identify the "plaintiff" and the "defendant." This may seem elementary and uncomplicated, but, especially in view of the creative editing practiced by some casebook editors, it is sometimes a difficult or even impossible task. Bear in mind that the *party presently* seeking something from this court may not be the plaintiff, and that sometimes only the cross-claim of a defendant is treated in the excerpt. Confusing or misaligning the parties can ruin your analysis and understanding of the case.

ISSUE: A statement of the general legal question answered by or illustrated in the case. For clarity, the issue is best put in the form of a question capable of a "yes" or "no" answer. In reality, the issue is simply the Rule of Law put in the form of a question (e.g., "May an offer be accepted by performance?").

The major problem presented in discerning what is *the* issue in the case is that an opinion usually purports to raise and answer several questions. However, except for rare cases, only one such question is really the issue in the case. Collateral issues not necessary to the resolution of the matter in controversy are handled by the court by language known as *"obiter dictum"* or merely *"dictum."* While dicta may be included later in the brief, they have no place under the issue heading.

To find the issue, ask *who wants what* and then go on to ask *why did that party succeed or fail in getting it*. Once this is determined, the "why" should be turned into a question.

The complexity of the issues in the cases will vary, but in all cases a single-sentence question should sum up the issue. *In a few cases,* there will be two, or even more rarely, three issues of equal importance to the resolution of the case. Each should be expressed in a single-sentence question.

Since many issues are resolved by a court in coming to a final disposition of a case, the casebook editor will reproduce the portion of the opinion containing the issue or issues most relevant to the area of law under scrutiny. A noted law professor gave this advice: "Close the book; look at the title on the cover." Chances are, if it is Property, you need not concern yourself with whether, for example, the federal government's treatment of the plaintiff's land really raises a federal question sufficient to support jurisdiction on this ground in federal court.

The same rule applies to chapter headings designating sub-areas within the subjects. They tip you off as to what the text is designed to teach. The cases are arranged in a casebook to show a progression or development of the law, so that the preceding cases may also help.

It is also most important to remember to *read the notes and questions* at the end of a case to determine what the editors wanted you to have gleaned from it.

HOLDING AND DECISION: This section should succinctly explain the rationale of the court in arriving at its decision. In capsulizing the "reasoning" of the court, it should always include an application of the general rule or rules of law to the specific facts of the case. Hidden justifications come to light in this entry: the reasons for the state of the law, the public policies, the biases and prejudices, those considerations that influence the justices' thinking and, ultimately, the outcome of the case. At the end, there should be a short indication of the disposition or procedural resolution of the case (e.g., "Decision of the trial court for Mr. Smith (P) reversed").

The foregoing format is designed to help you "digest" the reams of case material with which you will be faced in your law school career. Once mastered by practice, it will place at your fingertips the information the authors of your casebooks have sought to impart to you in case-by-case illustration and analysis.

B. Be as Economical as Possible in Briefing Cases

Once armed with a format that encourages succinctness, it is as important to be economical with regard to the time spent on the actual reading of the case as it is to be economical in the writing of the brief itself. This does not mean "skimming" a case. Rather, it means reading the case with an "eye" trained to recognize into which "section" of your brief a particular passage or line fits and having a system for quickly and precisely marking the case so that the passages fitting any one particular part of

the brief can be easily identified and brought together in a concise and accurate manner when the brief is actually written.

It is of no use to simply repeat everything in the opinion of the court; record only enough information to trigger your recollection of what the court said. Nevertheless, an accurate statement of the "law of the case," i.e., the legal principle applied to the facts, is absolutely essential to class preparation and to learning the law under the case method.

To that end, it is important to develop a "shorthand" that you can use to make marginal notations. These notations will tell you at a glance in which section of the brief you will be placing that particular passage or portion of the opinion.

Some students prefer to underline all the salient portions of the opinion (with a pencil or colored underliner marker), making marginal notations as they go along. Others prefer the color-coded method of underlining, utilizing different colors of markers to underline the salient portions of the case, each separate color being used to represent a different section of the brief. For example, blue underlining could be used for passages relating to the rule of law, yellow for those relating to the issue, and green for those relating to the holding and decision, etc. While it has its advocates, the color-coded method can be confusing and time-consuming (all that time spent on changing colored markers). Furthermore, it can interfere with the continuity and concentration many students deem essential to the reading of a case for maximum comprehension. In the end, however, it is a matter of personal preference and style. Just remember, whatever method you use, underlining must be used sparingly or its value is lost.

If you take the marginal notation route, an efficient and easy method is to go along underlining the key portions of the case and placing in the margin alongside them the following "markers" to indicate where a particular passage or line "belongs" in the brief you will write:

N   (NATURE OF CASE)
RL   (RULE OF LAW)
I   (ISSUE)
HL   (HOLDING AND DECISION, relates to the RULE OF LAW behind the decision)
HR   (HOLDING AND DECISION, gives the RATIONALE or reasoning behind the decision)
HA   (HOLDING AND DECISION, applies the general principle(s) of law to the facts of the case to arrive at the decision)

Remember that a particular passage may well contain information necessary to more than one part of your brief, in which case you simply note that in the margin. If you are using the color-coded underlining method instead of marginal notation, simply make asterisks or checks in the margin next to the passage in question in the colors that indicate the additional sections of the brief where it might be utilized.

The economy of utilizing "shorthand" in marking cases for briefing can be maintained in the actual brief writing process itself by utilizing "law student shorthand" within the brief. There are many commonly used words and phrases for which abbreviations can be substituted in your briefs (and in your class notes also). You can develop abbreviations that are personal to you and which will save you a lot of time. A reference list of briefing abbreviations can be found on page x of this book.

C. Use Both the Briefing Process and the Brief as a Learning Tool

Now that you have a format and the tools for briefing cases efficiently, the most important thing is to make the time spent in briefing profitable to you and to make the most advantageous use of the briefs you create. Of course, the briefs are invaluable for classroom reference when you are called upon to explain or analyze a particular

case. However, they are also useful in reviewing for exams. A quick glance at the fact summary should bring the case to mind, and a rereading of the rule of law should enable you to go over the underlying legal concept in your mind, how it was applied in that particular case, and how it might apply in other factual settings.

As to the value to be derived from engaging in the briefing process itself, there is an immediate benefit that arises from being forced to sift through the essential facts and reasoning from the court's opinion and to succinctly express them in your own words in your brief. The process ensures that you understand the case and the point that it illustrates, and that means you will be ready to absorb further analysis and information brought forth in class. It also ensures you will have something to say when called upon in class. The briefing process helps develop a mental agility for getting to the *gist* of a case and for identifying, expounding on, and applying the legal concepts and issues found there. The briefing process is the mental process on which you must rely in taking law school examinations; it is also the mental process upon which a lawyer relies in serving his clients and in making his living.

acceptance	acp	offer	O
affirmed	aff	offeree	OE
answer	ans	offeror	OR
assumption of risk	a/r	ordinance	ord
attorney	atty	pain and suffering	p/s
beyond a reasonable doubt	b/r/d	parol evidence	p/e
bona fide purchaser	BFP	plaintiff	P
breach of contract	br/k	prima facie	p/f
cause of action	c/a	probable cause	p/c
common law	c/l	proximate cause	px/c
Constitution	Con	real property	r/p
constitutional	con	reasonable doubt	r/d
contract	K	reasonable man	r/m
contributory negligence	c/n	rebuttable presumption	rb/p
cross	x	remanded	rem
cross-complaint	x/c	res ipsa loquitur	RIL
cross-examination	x/ex	respondeat superior	r/s
cruel and unusual punishment	c/u/p	Restatement	RS
defendant	D	reversed	rev
dismissed	dis	Rule Against Perpetuities	RAP
double jeopardy	d/j	search and seizure	s/s
due process	d/p	search warrant	s/w
equal protection	e/p	self-defense	s/d
equity	eq	specific performance	s/p
evidence	ev	statute	S
exclude	exc	statute of frauds	S/F
exclusionary rule	exc/r	statute of limitations	S/L
felony	f/n	summary judgment	s/j
freedom of speech	f/s	tenancy at will	t/w
good faith	g/f	tenancy in common	t/c
habeas corpus	h/c	tenant	t
hearsay	hr	third party	TP
husband	H	third party beneficiary	TPB
injunction	inj	transferred intent	TI
in loco parentis	ILP	unconscionable	uncon
inter vivos	I/v	unconstitutional	unconst
joint tenancy	j/t	undue influence	u/e
judgment	judgt	Uniform Commercial Code	UCC
jurisdiction	jur	unilateral	uni
last clear chance	LCC	vendee	VE
long-arm statute	LAS	vendor	VR
majority view	maj	versus	v
meeting of minds	MOM	void for vagueness	VFV
minority view	min	weight of authority	w/a
Miranda rule	Mir/r	weight of the evidence	w/e
Miranda warnings	Mir/w	wife	W
negligence	neg	with	w/
notice	ntc	within	w/i
nuisance	nus	without	w/o
obligation	ob	without prejudice	w/o/p
obscene	obs	wrongful death	wr/d

Table of Cases

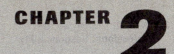

CHAPTER 2

Defining the Attorney-Client Relationship

Quick Reference Rules of Law

Perez v. Kirk & Carrigan

Truck driver (P) v. Attorneys (D)

Tex. Ct. App., 822 S.W.2d 261 (1991).

NATURE OF CASE: Appeal from summary judgment in action for breach of fiduciary duty, infliction of emotional distress, and consumer protection violations.

FACT SUMMARY: After Perez's (P) truck accident claimed the lives of 21 children, lawyers Kirk & Carrigan (D) disseminated to the district attorney's office the confidential statements Perez (P) made to them, resulting in Perez's (P) indictment.

RULE OF LAW
A lawyer may breach his fiduciary duty to his client either by wrongfully disclosing a privileged statement or by disclosing an unprivileged statement after wrongfully representing that it would be kept confidential.

FACTS: Perez (P), a truck driver for the Valley Coca-Cola Bottling Company, was in a traffic accident that resulted in the deaths of 21 children. Kirk & Carrigan (D), lawyers hired to represent Valley Coca-Cola Bottling Company, visited Perez (P) the day after the accident in the hospital and told him they were his lawyers too. Perez (P) gave a sworn statement to Kirk & Carrigan (D) with the understanding that the statement would be kept confidential. Soon thereafter, Kirk & Carrigan (D) voluntarily disclosed Perez's (P) statement to the district attorney's office under threat of subpoena. The district attorney's office obtained an indictment for involuntary manslaughter against Perez (P) based upon the statement. Perez (P) brought an action for breach of fiduciary duty against Kirk & Carrigan (D). Kirk & Carrigan (D) moved for summary judgment on the ground that the attorney-client privilege did not apply to Perez's (P) statement. The trial court granted summary judgment, and Perez (P) appealed.

ISSUE: Does a lawyer breach his fiduciary duty to maintain his client's confidences by disclosing an unprivileged statement after representing that it would be kept confidential?

HOLDING AND DECISION: (Dorsey, J.) Yes. A lawyer breaches his fiduciary duty to maintain his client's confidences by disclosing an unprivileged statement after representing that it would be kept confidential. Perez's (P) allegation here that Kirk & Carrigan (D) breached their fiduciary duty owed to him when they voluntarily disseminated his statement to the district attorney's office was a valid claim for damages for the emotional distress and mental anguish he suffered after being indicted. Once an attorney-client relationship arose between Kirk & Carrigan (D) and Perez (P), Kirk & Carigan (D) had a fiduciary and ethical duty not to disseminate statements Perez (P) made to them in confidence, regardless of whether the statements were privileged or not. The relationship between attorney and client requires absolute and perfect candor, openness and honesty, and the absence of any concealment or deception. Perez (P) has made a valid claim for damages. Reversed and remanded.

ANALYSIS

It is important to note that much information that is ethically protected will not be privileged. However, virtually all information considered privileged under the Rules of Evidence will also be ethically protected. A lawyer whom a court orders to reveal information that is ethically protected but not privileged under the Rules of Evidence will be required to reveal the information under pain of contempt. But if that lawyer had voluntarily revealed the same information, he or she might be guilty of a disciplinary violation for failure to protect a client's secrets or confidences, unless revelation was for one of the purposes recognized by DR 4-101 or Rule 1.6.

Quicknotes

ATTORNEY-CLIENT PRIVILEGE A doctrine precluding the admission into evidence of confidential communications between an attorney and his client made in the course of obtaining professional assistance.

FIDUCIARY DUTY A legal obligation to act for the benefit of another, including subordinating one's personal interests to that of the other person.

Upjohn Co. v. United States

Audited corporation (D) v. Internal Revenue Service (P)

449 U.S. 383 (1981).

NATURE OF CASE: Review of discovery order in tax investigation.

FACT SUMMARY: The Internal Revenue Service (IRS) (P), in a tax investigation of Upjohn Co. (D), sought disclosure of communications between middle- and lower-level employees and Upjohn's (D) attorneys.

RULE OF LAW

The attorney-client privilege between a corporation and its counsel extends to communications between counsel and noncontrol-level employees.

FACTS: The Internal Revenue Service (IRS) (P), in the course of a tax investigation of Upjohn Co. (D), sought disclosure of memoranda compiled by corporate attorneys during the course of their communications with nonsupervisory personnel. Upjohn (D) resisted, claiming the attorney-client privilege. The court of appeals held that the privilege applied only to communications between counsel and "control" employees, such as executives and senior management. The United States Supreme Court granted review.

ISSUE: Does the attorney-client privilege between a corporation and its counsel extend to communications between counsel and noncontrol-level employees?

HOLDING AND DECISION: (Rehnquist, J.) Yes. The attorney-client privilege between a corporation and its counsel extends to communications between counsel and noncontrol-level employees. The privilege exists largely because of recognition in the law that sound legal advice depends upon the lawyer being fully informed of relevant facts; if communications between a client and his counsel were discoverable, such communication would be largely circumscribed. In the context of a corporation, the information necessary for the corporation's attorneys to properly represent the corporation will not always come from the corporation's "control group"; often, the information will be in the possession of midlevel or even low-level employees. Communications between such employees and counsel may be no less necessary for proper representation, and therefore are no less deserving of confidentiality. Therefore, the privilege must be extended to all communications between counsel and corporate employees, no matter what level. Reversed.

ANALYSIS

It is important to note that the attorney-client privilege protects communications only, not information. While an attorney may not be compelled to disclose what a

corporate attorney communicated to him, the privilege does not bar the party seeking discovery from obtaining the information from the employee through a recognized discovery procedure such as a deposition. While it would be more convenient for the IRS (P), for example, to simply subpoena the notes taken by Upjohn's (D) attorney, the Court notes that considerations of convenience do not overcome the policies served by the attorney-client privilege.

Quicknotes

ATTORNEY-CLIENT PRIVILEGE A doctrine precluding the admission into evidence of confidential communications between an attorney and his client made in the course of obtaining professional assistance.

Taylor v. Illinois

Convicted criminal (D) v. Illinois (P)

484 U.S. 400 (1988).

NATURE OF CASE: Appeal from a criminal conviction.

FACT SUMMARY: Taylor (D) received a criminal conviction after the court refused to allow him to call a critical witness because his defense lawyer had failed to provide the prosecutor for the state of Illinois (P) with the name of the witness.

RULE OF LAW

The client must accept the consequences of the lawyer's decision to forgo cross-examination, to not put certain witnesses on the stand, or to not disclose the identity of certain witnesses in advance of trial.

FACTS: When Taylor's (D) lawyer refused to comply with the state prosecutor's (P) discovery request for the name of a witness pursuant to Illinois (P) discovery rules, the trial court judge refused to allow Taylor's (D) lawyer to call the witness whose testimony would have helped establish a defense of self-defense during the trial. Taylor (D) was convicted. Taylor's (D) conviction was upheld by the Illinois appellate courts, and Taylor (D) appealed to the United States Supreme Court, arguing that he should not be held responsible for his lawyer's misconduct.

ISSUE: When a lawyer decides to forgo cross-examination, to not put certain witnesses on the stand, or to not disclose the identity of certain witnesses in advance of trial, must a client accept the consequences of the lawyer's decision?

HOLDING AND DECISION: (Stevens, J.) Yes. The client must accept the consequences of the lawyer's decision to forgo cross-examination, to not put certain witnesses on the stand, or to not disclose the identity of certain witnesses in advance of trial. Taylor's (D) lawyer chose not to reveal his witness's identity until after the trial commenced. Taylor (D) has no right to disavow that decision now, absent ineffective assistance of counsel. Moreover, in responding to discovery, the client has a duty to be candid and forthcoming with the lawyer, and when the lawyer responds, he speaks for the client.

DISSENT: (Brennan, J.) In the absence of any evidence that a defendant played any part in an attorney's willful discovery violation, directly sanctioning the attorney is not only fairer but more effective in deterring violations than excluding defense evidence. While the court has sometimes held a defendant bound by tactical errors his attorney makes, we have not previously suggested that a client can be punished for an attorney's misconduct. There is no need to inflict punishment on the defendant because miscon-duct, not tactical errors, is amenable to direct punitive sanctions against attorneys as a deterrent that can prevent attorneys from systematically engaging in misconduct that would disrupt the trial process.

▶ ANALYSIS

This case stands for the proposition that lawyers are their clients' agents. As such, the lawyer must have full authority to manage the conduct of his client's case because it would be impracticable to require client approval of every tactical decision a lawyer may make. Consequently, the lawyer's conduct will be attributable to the client, even if the lawyer errs or is careless.

Quicknotes

ATTORNEY-CLIENT PRIVILEGE A doctrine precluding the admission into evidence of confidential communications between an attorney and his client made in the course of obtaining professional assistance.

INEFFECTIVE ASSISTANCE OF COUNSEL A claim brought by an accused in which it must be determined whether the attorney's rendering of representation was such that the ultimate disposition of the case may not be relied upon as fair.

Choice Hotels International, Inc. v. Grover

Franchisor (P) v. Franchisee investor (D)

792 F.3d 793 (7th Cir. 2015).

NATURE OF CASE: Appeal from denial of Fed. R. Civ. P. 60(b)(6) motion.

FACT SUMMARY: Grover (D) and partners (D) retained attorney Johnson to vacate a default judgment and defend against Choice Hotels' (P) damages claim. Johnson failed to do so and a new attorney filed a Fed. R. Civ. P. 60(b)(6) motion to set aside the final judgment.

🏛 RULE OF LAW
A final judgment in a civil litigation matter should not be disturbed due to ineffective counsel when a malpractice claim would compensate damaged litigants.

FACTS: Choice Hotels International, Inc. (P) filed a lawsuit against Tarranpaul Chawli, Anuj Grover, Arjun Grover, and Dharam Punwani (collectively, "Investors") (D) for damages arising out of an alleged breach of a franchise agreement. Chawli, a lawyer licensed in Illinois, initially represented the Investors (D), but failed to file responsive pleadings and the court entered a default judgment against the Investors (D). The Investors (D) hired new counsel, Elton Johnson, to vacate the default, negotiate a settlement, and defend against damages. Johnson did maintain limited communication with his clients and claimed he was negotiating a settlement, but he filed no motions or pleadings with the court. A final judgment awarded Choice Hotels (P) $430,286.75 in damages. Over one year later, the Investors (D) hired new counsel to replace Johnson and new counsel filed a Fed. R. Civ. P. 60(b)(6) motion to set aside the final judgment. A Rule 60 (b)(6) motion requires demonstration of "extraordinary circumstances" to grant relief from final judgment. Such relief is at the district court's discretion and review of the district court's decision is deferential to the district court. Here, the district court denied the motion finding no "extraordinary circumstances" in civil litigants having a poor lawyer. The court noted that a malpractice claim against Johnson was the remedy for legal neglect. [Investors (D) appealed.]

ISSUE: Should a final judgment in a civil litigation matter be disturbed due to ineffective counsel when a malpractice claim would compensate damaged litigants?

HOLDING AND DECISION: (Easterbrook, J.) No. A final judgment in a civil litigation matter should not be disturbed due to ineffective counsel when a malpractice claim would compensate damaged litigants. Investors (D) relied on *Holland v. Florida*, 560 U.S. 631 (2010), and *Maples v. Thomas*, 565 U.S. 266 (2012), to argue the Supreme Court has held abandonment by counsel permits additional federal review. Those cases were capital cases and appropriate holdings because death is a disproportionate penalty for having a bad lawyer. A malpractice claim would not right the wrong as it would in civil litigation. Civil litigants also can more easily than prisoners replace ineffective counsel. The Supreme Court has not indicated *Holland* or *Maples* extends to civil economic litigation. In those matters, a malpractice claim against the offending attorney should be adequate recompense. Litigants can ensure attorneys carry sufficient malpractice insurance before engagement if there is a concern there would be insufficient funds to compensate for legal malpractice. Civil litigants have an obligation to monitor their attorney and the failure to do so falls on them, not on the innocent adverse party. Johnson did not completely abandon the Investors (D) as he responded to a few emails and performed some tasks. Even if the court had found he abandoned the Investors (D), the group should have taken more affirmative steps to monitor the docket and confirm Johnson was filing appropriate motions. The district court did not abuse its discretion in denying their motion to set aside the final judgment. Affirmed.

▎ANALYSIS

Civil litigants have greater expectations placed upon them to monitor and direct their counsel. Judge Easterbrook does not express sympathy for those litigants who have no familiarity with the legal system, or limited time and resources to monitor counsel. He also does not address the additional time and expense a malpractice claim would require. When abandonment by counsel does not meet the standard to set aside a civil judgment, litigants have few alternatives but to carefully vet counsel prior to engagement. Litigants should ensure counsel carry sufficient malpractice insurance, have a consistent communication system in place to update clients, and express a willingness to explain the process the particular case will undergo.

■□■

Quicknotes

INEFFECTIVE ASSISTANCE OF COUNSEL A claim brought by an accused in which it must be determined whether the attorney's rendering of representation was such that the

Continued on next page.

ultimate disposition of the case may not be relied upon as fair.

MALPRACTICE A failure to perform one's professional duties during the course of a client relationship, either intentionally or negligently, or the poor or improper discharge of one's professional obligations.

Nichols v. Keller

Injured employee (P) v. Workers' compensation attorneys (D)

Cal. App. Ct., 15 Cal. App. 4th 1672, 19 Cal. Rptr. 2d 601 (1993).

NATURE OF CASE: Appeal from summary judgment dismissing malpractice action.

FACT SUMMARY: Fulfer & Keller (D) contended that they had not been obligated to advise client Nichols (P) of his civil suit remedies following a work-related injury because they represented him only on his workers' compensation claim.

RULE OF LAW

An attorney may be obligated to alert a client to legal remedies outside the direct scope of that attorney's representation of the client.

FACTS: Nichols (P) suffered a job-related injury. He retained Fulfer & Keller (D) to represent him in a workers' compensation claim. He did not learn of his potential recourse against third parties by way of civil suit until after the statute of limitations had passed. He sued Fulfer & Keller (D) for malpractice, contending that they had been under a duty to advise him of his rights with respect to a third-party suit. The trial court granted summary judgment dismissing the action, holding that Fulfer & Keller (D) did not owe Nichols (P) any such duty as it was not within the course of their representation. Nichols (P) appealed.

ISSUE: May an attorney be obligated to alert a client to legal remedies outside the direct scope of that attorney's representation of the client?

HOLDING AND DECISION: (Martin, J.) Yes. An attorney may be obligated to alert a client to legal remedies outside the direct scope of that attorney's representation of the client. One of the attorney's basic functions is to advise. Advice need not be on every possible alternative, but should cover all foreseeable negative consequences. If such a consequence is foreseeable even in an area outside the attorney's scope of representation, the attorney is still under a duty to disclose the risk. He can then advise the client that it is outside his expertise and/or scope of representation and that the client should seek other counsel, and then the onus is placed on the client to protect his rights. However, until this is done, it is the attorney's responsibility to inform the client of such rights. Here, even though Fulfer & Keller (D) represented Nichols (P) only on his workers' compensation claim, a civil suit was sufficiently related to the scope of the representation that Nichols (P) should at least have been advised that the remedy existed. Reversed.

▶ **ANALYSIS**

If there is one thing that gets lawyers in trouble with clients, it is lack of communication. Generally speaking, a lawyer can never disclose too much to a client; an attorney can, however, disclose too little, with consequences of the sort seen here. A good rule of thumb is "when in doubt, disclose."

Quicknotes

DUTY OF CARE A principle of negligence requiring an individual to act in such a manner as to avoid injury to a person to whom he or she owes an obligatory duty.

STATUTE OF LIMITATIONS A law prescribing the period in which a legal action may be commenced.

Jones v. Barnes

Public defender (D) v. Convicted robber (P)

463 U.S. 745 (1983).

NATURE OF CASE: Review of grant of habeas corpus.

FACT SUMMARY: Barnes (P) contended that he had an absolute right to have his attorney on appeal raise every nonfrivolous issue he requested.

RULE OF LAW
An attorney representing a defendant on appeal is not under a duty to raise every nonfrivolous issue requested by the defendant.

FACTS: Barnes (P) was convicted of armed robbery. A public defender was appointed to prosecute his appeal. Barnes (P) requested that certain issues be raised in the appeal. The attorney, for reasons of strategy, declined to press all the proffered issues. The conviction was affirmed. Barnes (P) petitioned for habeas corpus, contending that his attorney's refusal to prosecute all nonfrivolous issues constituted a denial of his Sixth Amendment right to counsel. The Second Circuit Court of Appeals granted the writ, and the United States Supreme Court granted review.

ISSUE: Is an attorney representing a defendant on appeal under a duty to raise every nonfrivolous issue requested by the defendant?

HOLDING AND DECISION: (Burger, C.J.) No. An attorney representing a defendant on appeal is not under a duty to raise every nonfrivolous issue requested by the defendant. It is safe to assume that counsel is in a better position than the defendant to assess how best to prosecute an appeal. In many situations, raising every issue will be detrimental to an appeal, as the weaker points will drown the stronger ones. To create a per se rule that a defendant is entitled to have appointed counsel raise every issue he wishes would seriously undermine the ability of counsel to present the client's case in accord with counsel's professional judgment. This Court is unwilling to take such a step. Reversed.

CONCURRENCE: (Blackmun, J.) An attorney may be ethically bound to raise all nonfrivolous issues requested by the client, but this duty does not rise to constitutional status.

DISSENT: (Brennan, J.) An appeal ultimately belongs to the defendant, and he must have the final say in how it is prosecuted.

ANALYSIS

It must be remembered that this was a constitutional ruling. The Court simply held that, as a matter of federal constitutional law, no right to press all issues on appeal belongs to one having appointed counsel. Depending on jurisdiction, an attorney may have an ethical obligation to prosecute all such issues. Canon 5 of the ABA Code of Professional Responsibility concerns an attorney's obligation to exercise independent professional judgment on behalf of such a client. This canon is primarily concerned with avoiding external, third-party influences over the attorney's decision-making process. It does not speak to interference by the client himself.

Quicknotes

HABEAS CORPUS A proceeding in which a defendant brings a writ to compel a judicial determination of whether he is lawfully being held in custody.

Olfe v. Gordon

Property seller (P) v. Real estate attorney (D)

Wis. Sup. Ct., 93 Wis. 2d 173, 286 N.W.2d 573 (1980).

NATURE OF CASE: Appeal of dismissal of action against an attorney by his former client.

FACT SUMMARY: A trial court held that expert testimony was required for Olfe (P) to recover against her former attorney, Gordon (D), even though he had intentionally disregarded her instructions in the underlying transaction.

 RULE OF LAW
When a client's attorney disregards his or her client's instructions to the client's detriment, expert testimony is not required for the client to recover.

FACTS: Olfe (P) retained Gordon (D), an attorney, to handle the sale of her house. She instructed him that she was willing to take back a first mortgage, but not a second mortgage. Nonetheless, Gordon (D) arranged a transaction that left Olfe (P) with a second mortgage, although Gordon (D) told her it was in fact a first mortgage. The purchaser defaulted, and the holder of the first mortgage foreclosed, extinguishing Olfe's (P) second mortgage. Olfe (P) lost about $25,000, and sued Gordon (D) to recover. After Olfe's (P) case, the court granted a nonsuit, on the basis that Olfe (P) had not provided expert testimony as to the standard of care required by attorneys in similar circumstances. Olfe (P) appealed.

ISSUE: When a client's attorney disregards his or her client's instructions to the client's detriment, is expert testimony required for the client to recover?

HOLDING AND DECISION: [Judge not stated in casebook excerpt.] No. When a client's attorney disregards his or her client's instructions to the detriment of the client, expert testimony is not required for the client to recover. It has generally been recognized that an attorney may be liable for all losses caused by his failure to follow with reasonable promptness and care the explicit instructions of his or her client. Moreover, an attorney's honest belief that the instructions were not in the best interests of the client provides no defense to a suit for malpractice. The attorney-client relationship in such contexts is one of agent to principal, and an agent is answerable to that principal for failure to follow instructions. A cause of action in this situation may be based upon fiduciary principles, upon contract, or in tort. In any event, expert testimony is not needed, as a lay jury is perfectly capable of understanding on its own whether an attorney failed to follow instructions. Reversed.

▶ ANALYSIS

The ABA Code of Professional Responsibility does not say in so many words that an attorney is duty-bound to follow his or her client's instructions. Canon 7 does require an attorney to represent a client zealously, but no mandate regarding instructions is made. The rule here is more a product of agency law than the code of ethics.

Quicknotes

AGENCY A fiduciary relationship whereby authority is granted to an agent to act on behalf of the principal in order to effectuate the principal's objective.

DUTY OF CARE A principle of negligence requiring an individual to act in such a manner as to avoid injury to a person to whom he or she owes an obligatory duty.

Protecting the Attorney-Client Relationship Against Outside Interference

Quick Reference Rules of Law

PAGE

1. *Niesig v. Team I.* An attorney may conduct ex parte interviews with a corporate adversary's current employees if the employees do not have power to bind the corporation. 12

2. *United States v. Carona.* Prosecutors do not violate their ethical obligations by communicating pre-indictment with an attorney-represented defendant through a cooperating witness who uses falsified documents provided by the prosecution to obtain evidence from the defendant. 13

3. *In re Eisenstein.* Counsel in receipt of mistakenly sent or procured evidence must promptly notify the sender so protective measures can be taken. 15

Niesig v. Team I

Injured construction worker (P) v. [Party not identified.] (D)

N.Y. Ct. App., 76 N.Y.2d 363, 558 N.E.2d 1030, 559 N.Y.S.2d 493 (1990).

NATURE OF CASE: Appeal of ruling on motion to permit ex parte interviews.

FACT SUMMARY: Niesig's (P) attorney wished to conduct interviews with employees of DeTrae Enterprises, Inc. (D) without the presence of DeTrae's (D) counsel.

🏛 RULE OF LAW
An attorney may conduct ex parte interviews with a corporate adversary's current employees if the employees do not have power to bind the corporation.

FACTS: Niesig (P) was injured on a construction site. He sued various entities. Joined as a third-party defendant was his employer, DeTrae Enterprises, Inc. (D). Niesig's (P) attorney, wishing to conduct ex parte interviews with DeTrae (D) employee-witnesses, moved the court for an order approving such action. [The casebook excerpt did not state the trial court ruling.] The appellate division held that current employees were "parties" and therefore could not be communicated with directly. The New York Court of Appeals, the state's highest court, granted review.

ISSUE: May an attorney conduct ex parte interviews with a corporate adversary's current employees if the employees do not have power to bind the corporation?

HOLDING AND DECISION: (Kaye, J.) Yes. An attorney may conduct ex parte interviews with a corporate adversary's current employees if the employees do not have power to bind the corporation. Disciplinary Rule 7-104(A)(1) of the New York Code of Professional Responsibility contains the universal prohibition against communicating with opposing "parties." When opponents are corporations, the question arises as to who will be considered a "party," as a corporation can only act through individuals. As the Code of Professional Responsibility is not a statute, the courts do not have to give effect to any legislative intent and can interpret the rule as they see fit. One interpretation urged, which is rejected, would hold all employees to be covered. This is unsatisfactory because it would preclude informal discovery, which is an expedient way of helping to resolve disputes. Another interpretation would be the so-called "control group" test, which holds that only controlling individuals in a corporation (usually executives) would be covered by the rule. This rule wholly overlooks the fact that corporate employees other than senior management can speak for a corporation. The best rule is one that includes all persons who have authority to bind the corporation. This test will not be hard to apply, as it is grounded in principles of agency and evidence that are well known to attorneys. This rule is

different than the one issued by the appellate division, so its order is modified and the matter remanded.

▶ ANALYSIS

The court here partially based its decision upon rules of evidence, although it did not specify the rules to which it was referring. In fact, at least at the federal level, evidentiary rules are different. For instance, the attorney-client privilege applies to all employees, not just "alter ego" employees.

Quicknotes

ATTORNEY-CLIENT PRIVILEGE A doctrine precluding the admission into evidence of confidential communications between an attorney and his client made in the course of obtaining professional assistance.

EX PARTE A proceeding commenced by one party without providing any opposing parties with notice or which is uncontested by an adverse party.

NEW YORK CODE OF PROFESSIONAL RESPONSIBILITY DR 7-104(A)(1) Prohibits a lawyer from communicating directly with a party known to have counsel in the matter.

United States v. Carona

Federal government (P) v. Corrupt sheriff (D)

660 F.3d 360 (9th Cir. 2011).

NATURE OF CASE: Appeal from conviction for witness tampering.

FACT SUMMARY: The district court held that federal prosecutors (P) violated Cal. R. Professional Conduct 2-100 by communicating with Carona (D), a former sheriff accused of various federal crimes and known by the prosecutors (P) to be represented by counsel, through Haidl, a cooperating witness, whom prosecutors (P) had given fake documents to use in eliciting incriminating statements.

RULE OF LAW

Prosecutors do not violate their ethical obligations by communicating pre-indictment with an attorney-represented defendant through a cooperating witness who uses falsified documents provided by the prosecution to obtain evidence from the defendant.

FACTS: Carona (D) had been the sheriff of Orange County, California, from 1999 to 2008, when he resigned after being indicted on various federal corruption charges. During his initial campaign for sheriff in 1998, Carona (D) received financial support from Haidl to whom Carona (D) had offered the complete power of the sheriff's department in exchange for raising money and supporting Carona (D). After Carona (D) was elected, Haidl continued to make illicit payments to Carona (D), and he also gave Carona (D) a speedboat, which they concealed via a sham transaction. The federal government (P) started an investigation into Carona's (D) corruption in 2004, and in 2007, Haidl admitted his guilt and signed a cooperation plea agreement with the government (P). Following this plea agreement, government attorneys (P) instructed Haidl to meet with Carona (D) and to make surreptitious recordings of their meetings. At this time, Carona (D) was represented by attorney Stewart, who had notified the government (P) that he was representing Carona (D). After two meetings between Haidl and Carona (D) that failed to yield adequate evidence, prosecutors (P) equipped Haidl with two fake "subpoena attachments" that identified certain records that Haidl was to tell Carona (D) he had been subpoenaed to produce. These documents referred to cash payments Haidl provided to Carona (D) and to the sham transaction they used to conceal the gift of the speedboat. At the next meeting between Haidl and Carona (D), Carona (D) made statements that suggested both that he had received payments and gifts from Haidl and that he wanted Haidl to lie to the grand jury about these transactions. Carona (D) was subsequently convicted of witness tampering. The

district court, which had ruled that the prosecution (P) had violated Cal. R. Professional Conduct 2-100 by communicating with Carona (D) through Haidl, even though Carona (D) was known to be represented by counsel, nevertheless refused to suppress the evidence so obtained, instead leaving the matter for California's disciplinary authorities. The court of appeals granted review.

ISSUE: Do prosecutors violate their ethical obligations by communicating pre-indictment with an attorney-represented defendant through a cooperating witness who uses falsified documents provided by the prosecution to obtain evidence from the defendant?

HOLDING AND DECISION: (Clifton, J.) No. Prosecutors do not violate their ethical obligations by communicating pre-indictment with an attorney-represented defendant through a cooperating witness who uses falsified documents provided by the prosecution to obtain evidence from the defendant. Whether pre-indictment, non-custodial communications by federal prosecutors and investigators with represented parties violates Rule 2-100 is decided on a case-by-case basis. Precedent has more often than not held that specific instances of contact between undercover agents or cooperating witnesses and represented suspects do not violate Rule 2-100. The added wrinkle in this case is that here the prosecutors (P) provided Haidl with fake subpoena attachments to use in getting Carona (D) to incriminate himself. The district court held that this made Haidl the alter ego of the prosecutors (P), causing Haidl's communication with Carona (D) to violate Rule 2-100. The district court's ruling was erroneous because the use of the fake court papers did not cause Haidl to be any more an alter ego of the prosecutor (P) than he already was by agreeing to work with the prosecutor (P). The fake documents were mere props, and it has long been established that the government (P) may use deception in its investigations in order to induce suspects into making incriminating statements. The district court's concern that a suspect might be tricked by counsel's artful examination is inapplicable here, since Carona (D) was not subject to any interrogation, let alone one by the prosecutor (P). Rather he was engaging in a conversation with an individual he believed to be his ally. Finally, it would be antithetical to the administration of justice to allow a wrongdoer to immunize himself against such undercover operations simply by letting it be known that he has retained counsel, especially where, as here, the defendant has encouraged others to lie to the grand jury.

Continued on next page.

For all these reasons, as presented by the particular facts of this case, there was no violation of Rule 2-100. Affirmed.

▶ *ANALYSIS*

The district court had based its finding that there had been a violation of the no-contact rule on the Second Circuit's decision in *United States v. Hammad*, 858 F.2d 834 (2d Cir. 1988), which held that issuing a false subpoena to an informant to "create a pretense that might help the informant elicit admissions . . . contributed to the informant's becoming that alter ego of the prosecutor." The court in this case, rejecting the *Hammad* rationale, concluded that the fake court papers did not render Haidl the prosecutor's (P) alter ego, reasoning that "If government officials may pose as non-existent sheiks in an elaborately concocted scheme, supply a necessary ingredient for a drug operation, and utilize landing strips, docking facilities, and other accouterments of an organized smuggling operation, all in order to catch criminals, then their use of a subpoena in the name of an undercover agent to enable him to retain his credibility with suspected criminals seems innocuous by comparison." No precedent from any circuit, with the exception of *Hammad*, has held such indirect contacts to violate Rule 2-100 or similar rules.

■■■

Quicknotes

SUBPOENA A command issued by court to compel a witness to appear at trial.

■■■

In re Eisenstein

Attorney (D)

Mo. Sup. Ct., 485 S.W.3d 759 (2016).

NATURE OF CASE: Disciplinary action.

FACT SUMMARY: Eisenstein (D) faced disciplinary action against his license to practice law for his alleged violation of Rule 4-4.4(a) related to improperly obtaining evidence.

 RULE OF LAW
Counsel in receipt of mistakenly sent or procured evidence must promptly notify the sender so protective measures can be taken.

FACTS: Eisenstein (D) represented Husband in a dissolution of Husband's marriage to Wife. Husband accessed Wife's personal email account without her knowledge or permission. He obtained her payroll records and the direct testimony outline emailed to her by Wife's attorney, Stephanie Jones. Husband gave these documents to Eisenstein (D), but Eisenstein (D) did not notify Jones. On the second day of trial, Eisenstein (D) provided Jones a stack of exhibits, including the payroll records and direct testimony outline. Jones subsequently requested a conference with the judge and a hearing on the record. During the hearing, Eisenstein (D) testified he looked at the documents upon receipt from Husband, recognized them as "verboten," but did not alert Jones about the documents or that Husband accessed Wife's account. He admitted he teased Jones about the objections he planned to make to her direct examination questions.

ISSUE: Must counsel in receipt of mistakenly sent or procured evidence promptly notify the sender so protective measures can be taken?

HOLDING AND DECISION: (Teitelman, J.) Yes. Counsel in receipt of mistakenly sent or procured evidence must promptly notify the sender so protective measures can be taken. Eisenstein (D) is alleged to have violated Rule 4-4.4(a), which is meant to prevent "unwarranted intrusions into privileged relationships, such as the client-lawyer relationship." The evidence supports a finding that Eisenstein (D) violated this rule when he accepted and retained documents, including a direct testimony outline, without promptly notifying Jones. Jones testified Eisenstein (D) referenced Wife's payroll records during pretrial settlement negotiations. Eisenstein (D) conceded he knew the documents Husband obtained were "verboten" but he failed to immediately disclose his possession to Jones until after the start of the trial. Eisenstein (D) argues he did not behave improperly because it was Husband who accessed Wife's account. Rule 4-4.4, however, requires attorneys in possession of documents mistakenly sent or procured to promptly notify the sender so protective measures can be taken. Eisenstein (D) did not promptly notify Jones. Eisenstein (D) is suspended indefinitely with leave to reapply after six months. [Two judges would have required a 12-month suspension prior to reapplication.]

▌ANALYSIS

Attorneys cannot hide behind their clients who improperly obtain evidence because the rules put the burden on the receiving attorneys to promptly notify the proper parties regardless of the method the documents were obtained. The rule discourages attorneys from turning a blind eye to others' bad acts and using the improperly obtained evidence.

■□■

Lawyers, Money, and the Ethics of Legal Fees

Quick Reference Rules of Law

Brobeck, Phleger & Harrison v. Telex Corp.

Law firm (P) v. Computer corporation (D)

602 F.2d 866 (9th Cir.), *cert. denied*, 444 U.S. 981 (1979).

NATURE OF CASE: Appeal of award of damages for breach of contract.

FACT SUMMARY: Telex Corp. (D) contended that a contingency fee of $1,000,000 for the handling of a writ of certiorari to the United States Supreme Court was unconscionable.

🏛 RULE OF LAW
A contingency fee of $1,000,000 for handling a writ of certiorari to the United States Supreme Court is not unconscionable.

FACTS: Telex Corp. (D) filed an antitrust action against International Business Machines, Inc. (IBM). It recovered $259,500,000, but IBM recovered $18,500,000 by way of counterclaim. On appeal, the court of appeals reversed Telex's (D) award but affirmed that of IBM. Telex (D) engaged the firm of Brobeck, Phleger & Harrison (Brobeck) (P), a preeminent antitrust litigation firm, to handle a writ of certiorari to the Supreme Court. The fee arrangement called for a $25,000 retainer with a 5 percent contingency provision, the contingency in no event to be less than $1,000,000 in the event of a successful conclusion. [Telex (D) later denied that this had been the arrangement.] The petition was filed. Brobeck (P) eventually worked out a "wash" settlement wherein the writ would be dismissed in exchange for a dismissal of the counterclaim. Brobeck (P) then submitted a bill for $1,000,000, which Telex (D) refused to pay. Brobeck (P) sued for breach of contract. The district court awarded $1,000,000. Telex (D) appealed, contending that (1) the amount awarded did not reflect the terms of the contract, and (2) the amount of the contract was unconscionable.

ISSUE: Is a contingency fee of $1,000,000 for handling a writ of certiorari to the United States Supreme Court unconscionable?

HOLDING AND DECISION: (Per curiam) No. A contingency fee of $1,000,000 for handling a writ of certiorari to the United States Supreme Court is not unconscionable. [The Court first decided that the award did in fact reflect the terms of the contract.] A contract will be unconscionable only if it is one that "no man in his senses and not under a delusion would make on the one hand, and no honest man would accept on the other." Such an analysis will naturally depend on the facts of the case. In this instance the client, Telex (D), was faced with a large judgment that apparently jeopardized its continued corporate existence. It engaged the services of a high-profile law firm, whose engagement was almost surely one of the reasons IBM was willing to dismiss its judgment in exchange for a dismissal of the certiorari petition. Under these circumstances, the retainer agreement cannot be said to fall within the test above. This is particularly true in light of the fact Telex (D) in no way could have been considered an unsophisticated client. Affirmed.

▶ ANALYSIS

DR 2-106 of the ABA Code of Professional Responsibility provides, "A lawyer shall not enter into an agreement for, charge, or collect an illegal or clearly excessive fee." The Rule goes on to list certain factors to be considered in determining whether a fee is clearly excessive. Of particular importance was the factor enumerated in DR 2-106(B)(7): "[T]he experience, reputation, and ability of the lawyer or lawyers performing the services." In this instance, Telex (D) wanted and got the best, and for that it had to pay.

━━■

Quicknotes

PETITION FOR CERTIORARI A written request submitted to an appellate court asking that court to hear an appeal from an action in a lower court.

UNCONSCIONABILITY Rule of law whereby a court may excuse performance of a contract, or of a particular contract term, if it determines that such term(s) are unduly oppressive or unfair to one party to the contract.

━━■

In re Laurence S. Fordham

State bar (P) v. Attorney (D)

Mass. Sup. Jud. Ct., 423 Mass. 481, 668 N.E.2d 816 (1996), *cert. denied*, 519 U.S. 1149 (1997).

NATURE OF CASE: Appeal from a ruling for defendant in case alleging excessive fees were charged by an attorney.

FACT SUMMARY: Fordham (D), an attorney representing a client charged with driving under the influence of alcohol, allegedly charged an excessively high fee.

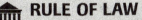

RULE OF LAW
In determining whether fees are clearly excessive, a court may examine the difficulty of the issues presented, the time and skill required to perform the legal service properly, and the fee customarily charged in the locality for comparable services.

FACTS: The father of an accused drunk driver hired Fordham (D), an experienced litigator in a prestigious Boston law firm, to handle the case, but later refused to pay the fees charged. Bar counsel (P) charged Fordham (D) with charging a clearly excessive fee under Disciplinary Rule (DR) 2-106(A). Fordham (D) alleged that dishonesty, bad faith or overreaching must be shown for discipline of an attorney. The hearing committee found that Fordham's (D) fee fell within a safe harbor because an agreement existed between a client and an attorney, which protected from challenge the contention that the fee was clearly excessive. Bar counsel (P) appealed to the Supreme Judicial Court.

ISSUE: In determining whether fees are clearly excessive, may a court examine the difficulty of the issues presented, the time and skill required to perform the legal service properly, and the fee customarily charged in the locality for comparable services?

HOLDING AND DECISION: (O'Connor, J.) Yes. In determining whether fees are clearly excessive, a court may examine the difficulty of the issues presented, the time and skill required to perform the legal service properly, and the fee customarily charged in the locality for comparable services. The hearing committee's and the board's determinations that a clearly excessive fee was not charged were not warranted. The amount of time Fordham (D) spent to educate himself and represent his client was excessive despite his good faith and diligence. DR 2-106(B)'s mandate, by referring to a lawyer of ordinary prudence, creates explicitly an objective standard by which attorneys' fees are to be judged. Dishonesty, bad faith or overreaching need not be established for discipline to be necessary. A public reprimand is the appropriate sanction for charging a clearly

excessive fee. Such a sanction is appropriate in this case. Reversed.

ANALYSIS

The court in this case considered eight factors to ascertain the reasonableness of the fee. The first factor required examining the time and labor required, the novelty and difficulty of the questions involved, and the skill requisite to perform the legal service properly. Another factor considered was the fee customarily charged in the locality for similar legal services. ABA Model Rule 1.5(a) is the modern equivalent to the Mode Code DR2-106(B).

Quicknotes

PUBLIC REPRIMAND An official warning or admonition.

Goldfarb v. Virginia State Bar

Real estate lawyers (P) v. State bar association (D)

421 U.S. 773 (1975).

NATURE OF CASE: Review of order dismissing class action seeking damages and injunctive relief under federal antitrust laws.

FACT SUMMARY: The Goldfarbs (P) contended that a minimum-fee schedule published by the Virginia State Bar (D) constituted price fixing in violation of the Sherman Act.

🏛 RULE OF LAW
Minimum fees mandated by a state bar may constitute price fixing in violation of the Sherman Act.

FACTS: The Goldfarbs (P) sought to engage a lawyer to do a title search on the home they wished to purchase. Per state law, only an attorney could do this. They consulted numerous attorneys, none of whom was willing to do the task for less than the minimum fee published by the Virginia State Bar (D). The Goldfarbs (P) subsequently brought a class action suit, contending that the minimum fee schedule constituted price fixing in violation of the Sherman Antitrust Act. The court of appeals held it was not, and dismissed. The United States Supreme Court granted review.

ISSUE: May minimum fees mandated by a state bar violate the Sherman Act?

HOLDING AND DECISION: (Burger, C.J.) Yes. Minimum fees mandated by a state bar may constitute price fixing in violation of the Sherman Act. To constitute a violation, the minimum fee schedule must amount to price fixing affecting interstate commerce, and not be subject to an exemption to the Sherman Act. A purely advisory fee schedule would present a different situation, but the record here reveals that attorneys in Virginia are under considerable pressure not to violate the State Bar's (D) fixed, rigid price floor. This being so, the schedule of minimum fees does constitute price fixing. It clearly affects interstate commerce. The Bar (D) argues that an exception should be made for "learned professions." The problem with this argument is that no such exception exists in the Sherman Act. As the Act is expressly designed to reach as broadly as possible, courts should not create exceptions not found in the Act's text. Finally, the Bar (D) argues that the fee schedule does fall within an exception for state action. The record here, however, belies this assertion. The State Bar (D) is not a governmental entity, but a private association to whom some regulatory oversight has been delegated. It is not an arm of either the executive or judicial branches of the state. If the state wanted to directly regulate

fees, it could do so. It has not so done, however, so the exception is inapplicable. Therefore, since the fee schedule does constitute price fixing affecting interstate commerce and no exception applies, it violates the Sherman Act. Reversed and remanded.

▶ ANALYSIS

In the 1970s, the United States Supreme Court began to whittle away at some of the powers that state bars once had to regulate the commercial aspect of lawyer behavior. Fee setting is an example. Another is lawyer advertising. Interestingly, Chief Justice Burger, who wrote the present opinion, was the most vociferous dissenter in the cases that liberalized lawyer advertising.

Quicknotes

MINIMUM FEE SCHEDULES The publication of recommended fee rates to be charged by attorneys; such fee schedules are in violation of federal antitrust laws.

STATE ACTION Actions brought pursuant to the Fourteenth Amendment claiming that the government violated the plaintiff's civil rights.

Evans v. Jeff D.

N/A

475 U.S. 717 (1986).

NATURE OF CASE: Review of invalidation of fee waiver.

FACT SUMMARY: A consent decree ending a civil rights action contained a waiver of statutory attorney fees, a provision invalidated on appeal.

RULE OF LAW
A consent decree ending a civil rights action may contain a fee waiver.

FACTS: A class of plaintiffs filed a civil rights action against various Idaho officials, contending discrimination against those with certain handicaps. The class was represented by Johnson, a public-interest attorney. Near the time of trial, the state officials made an offer of prospective relief basically giving the plaintiff class all it wanted. The only condition was a waiver of fees awardable under 42 U.S.C. § 1988. The plaintiffs agreed, and a consent decree, including approval of the fee waiver, was entered. Johnson then filed an appeal, contending that such waivers were void as contrary to statute and legal ethics. The Ninth Circuit Court of Appeals reversed the approval of the fee waiver, holding it invalid. The state officials petitioned for certiorari.

ISSUE: May a consent decree ending a civil rights action contain a fee waiver?

HOLDING AND DECISION: (Stevens, J.) Yes. A consent decree ending a civil rights action may contain a fee waiver. The text of the Fees Act, codified at 42 U.S.C. § 1988, provides no support for the proposition that Congress intended to ban all fee waivers offered in connection with substantial relief on the merits. The language clearly makes the award of fees discretionary, not mandatory. Further, to hold that waivers are per se invalid would, at least in some cases, run contrary to the intent of the statute, which is promotion of the vindication of civil rights. This is because knowledge that settlement would necessarily involve attorney fees would make settlement less attractive and, therefore, force a trial in some cases where it could have been avoided. Therefore, the better rule is that whether or not a fee waiver will be allowed in any consent decree will be left to the sound discretion of the trial court. [The Court went on to hold that the district court had not abused its discretion in approving the fee waiver.] Reversed.

DISSENT: (Brennan, J.) It is true that neither the language nor the history of 42 U.S.C. § 1988 would tend to preclude fee waivers. It is quite likely that the drafters gave the matter no thought at all. However, the effect of this decision will be to make lawyers more reluctant to take civil rights cases, which is clearly contrary to the intent behind the section. An attorney is ethically bound to accept his client's decision regarding settlement, and knowing that such a decision may end up in noncompensation will certainly not work in favor of an attorney taking a case.

ANALYSIS

The dissent and the majority opinion took entirely different approaches to the issue here. The majority opinion saw this as a straightforward matter of statutory construction. The dissent saw it not only as a statutory issue, but a matter of ethics as well, implicating Ethical Considerations 7-7 and 7-9 of the ABA Model Code of Responsibility.

Quicknotes

CONSENT DECREE A decree issued by a court of equity ratifying an agreement between the parties to a lawsuit; an agreement by a defendant to cease illegal activity.

WAIVER The intentional or voluntary forfeiture of a recognized right.

CHAPTER 5

Concurrent Conflicts of Interest

Quick Reference Rules of Law

In re Neville

N/A

Ariz. Sup. Ct., 147 Ariz. 106, 708 P.2d 1297 (1985).

NATURE OF CASE: Appeal from disciplinary action.

FACT SUMMARY: Attorney Neville (D) entered into a real estate transaction with Bly (P), his client, and a third party in which Bly (P) claimed the terms of the contract were adverse to his interest.

🏛 RULE OF LAW
Whenever lawyers knowingly acquire an ownership, possessory, security, or other pecuniary interest adverse to a client, the client must be given a reasonable opportunity to seek the advice of independent counsel.

FACTS: Attorney Neville (D) represented Bly (P), a licensed real estate broker, in certain real estate matters. Neville (D) also purchased options in certain of Bly's (P) properties. Neville (D), Bly (P), and a third party then entered into a contract, drafted by Neville (D), under which one of the Bly (P) properties would go to Neville (D) in exchange for a promissory note. Bly (P) created the substantive terms, and Neville (D) accepted these terms with no negotiation. The Arizona Bar charged Neville (D) with violation of Disciplinary Rule (DR) 5-104(A), the rule governing attorney-client business deals.

ISSUE: When lawyers knowingly acquire an ownership, possessory, security, or other pecuniary interest adverse to a client, must the client be given a reasonable opportunity to seek the advice of independent counsel?

HOLDING AND DECISION: (Feldman, J.) Yes. Whenever lawyers knowingly acquire an ownership, possessory, security, or other pecuniary interest adverse to a client, the client must be given a reasonable opportunity to seek the advice of independent counsel. In this case, Neville (D) was engaged in a business transaction in which his interests were adverse to those of his client, Bly (P), without giving Bly (P) a reasonable opportunity to seek the advice of independent counsel. DR 5-104 is applicable even in situations in which the attorney did not intend to defraud or act with improper motives. The application of DR 5-104 is not limited to those situations in which the lawyer is acting as counsel in the very transaction in which his interests are adverse to his client. It applies also to transactions in which, although the lawyer is not formally in an attorney-client relationship with the adverse party, it may fairly be said that because of other transactions, an ordinary person would look to the lawyer as a protector rather than as an adversary. Affirmed.

▶ ANALYSIS

The courts are very suspicious of business deals between attorneys and clients, a suspicion that led to the drafting of Rule 1.8(a) and DR 5-104(A). The courts scrutinize such transactions closely despite the fact lawyers are provided no bright line by which to determine when they can act as ordinary businesspeople in relation to the interests of those whom they have represented in the past or whom they represent on other matters at the present. The courts make it more difficult for lawyers to deal adversely with past and present clients because it is believed that this result conforms to the obligation of the profession and is in the public interest.

Quicknotes

FIDUCIARY DUTY A legal obligation to act for the benefit of another, including subordinating one's personal interests to that of the other person.

Cuyler v. Sullivan

[Party not identified.] (P) v. Convicted murderer (D)

446 U.S. 335 (1980).

NATURE OF CASE: Review of habeas corpus granted subsequent to murder conviction.

FACT SUMMARY: Sullivan (D), convicted of murder, was granted habeas corpus because the court found the possibility of conflict in his representation.

RULE OF LAW
The mere potential of a conflict of interest in representation is not sufficient to invalidate a conviction.

FACTS: Sullivan (D) was accused of murder, along with two accomplices. Sullivan (D) was tried separately, his trial occurring first. He was represented by two attorneys, who also represented the accomplices. His attorneys rested without presenting evidence. Sullivan (D) was convicted. He appealed, contending that a conflict of interest existed as to his representation. The conviction was affirmed. Sullivan (D) petitioned for habeas corpus. At a hearing, one attorney testified that the decision not to present a case was due to a weak state case. The other testified that he didn't wish to reveal the testimony of certain witnesses, in view of the upcoming trial of the accomplices. The district court denied habeas corpus, but the court of appeals reversed, holding that since a possibility of conflict existed, Sullivan (D) had been denied effective counsel. The United States Supreme Court granted review.

ISSUE: Is the mere potential of a conflict of interest in representation sufficient to invalidate a conviction?

HOLDING AND DECISION: (Powell, J.) No. The mere potential of a conflict of interest in representation is not sufficient to invalidate a conviction. The potential for a conflict of interest exists in every situation involving multiple representation, so to hold that the mere potential of a conflict is sufficient to invalidate a conviction would end multiple representation. However, in many cases multiple representation actually improves the position of the defendant. In light of this, this Court believes that only an actual conflict, as opposed to a potential conflict, should invalidate a conviction. Prejudice is presumed when a conflict exists, but should not be when one is only possible. Reversed and remanded.

CONCURRENCE: (Brennan, J.) A court should undertake its own inquiry as to whether a conflict exists.

CONCURRENCE AND DISSENT: (Marshall, J.) The trial court has a duty to ascertain that multiple representation is the product of the defendant's informed choice.

ANALYSIS

No objection was made by Sullivan (D) to multiple representation in the underlying trial. In his habeas corpus petition, Sullivan (D) contended that a court should undertake its own investigation to determine the potential for conflicts. Justices Brennan and Marshall took exception to the Court's ruling in this regard.

Quicknotes

CONFLICT OF INTEREST Refers to ethical problems that arise, or may be anticipated to arise, between an attorney and his client if the interests of the attorney, another client or a third party conflict with those of the present client.

HABEAS CORPUS A proceeding in which a defendant brings a writ to compel a judicial determination of whether he is lawfully being held in custody.

Wheat v. United States

Drug conspirator (D) v. Federal government (P)

486 U.S. 153 (1988).

NATURE OF CASE: Appeal from conviction for federal narcotics laws violations.

FACT SUMMARY: Ruling that a conflict existed, the district court refused to allow Wheat (D) to retain the same counsel who was representing Wheat's (D) codefendants.

🏛 RULE OF LAW
If a trial court believes that representation of a defendant by an attorney presents a serious potential for conflict, the court may refuse to permit that representation, even in the face of a waiver.

FACTS: Wheat (D) was indicted, along with Gomez-Barajas (D) and Bravo (D), for violation of federal narcotics laws. Shortly before his trial, Wheat (D) requested that the court allow him to substitute in as counsel of record Iredale, who also represented Gomez-Barajas (D) and Bravo (D), who had pleaded guilty but whose plea bargains had not as yet been accepted. The government (P) objected, contending that if the court elected not to permit Gomez-Barajas's (D) and Bravo's (D) plea bargains, Wheat (D) would almost certainly be called as witness at their subsequent trials. This would, said the government (P), put Iredale in conflict among his clients. Wheat (D) offered a waiver. Nonetheless, the court, finding strong probability of conflict, refused to allow Iredale to substitute in. Wheat (D) was convicted, and he appealed, contending he had been denied the right to counsel per the Sixth Amendment. The court of appeals affirmed, and the United States Supreme Court granted review.

ISSUE: If a trial court believes that representation of a defendant by an attorney presents a serious potential for conflict, may the court refuse to permit the representation, even in the face of a waiver?

HOLDING AND DECISION: (Rehnquist, C.J.) Yes. If a trial court believes that representation of a defendant by an attorney presents a serious potential for conflict, the court may refuse to permit that representation, even in the face of a waiver. The Sixth Amendment guarantees the right to effective counsel, not the right to counsel of choice. The guiding purpose behind the Amendment is to ensure a fair trial. While this goal has been interpreted to create a presumption in favor of permitting a party to retain counsel of choice, if the exercise of such choice leads to the potential for a fair trial to be unlikely, this presumption must give way. The possibility of waiver does not alter this conclusion. Courts have an interest in being sustained on appeal, and appellate courts can and do find waivers

invalid in ineffective-assistance-of-counsel claims. The decision of whether to permit a representation that poses a threat of conflict is best made by the trial court, and nothing in the record here shows that the district court violated the standards articulated above. Affirmed.

DISSENT: (Marshall, J.) The propriety of the district court's order thus depends on whether the government (P) showed that the particular facts and circumstances of the multiple representation proposed in this case were such as to overcome the presumption in favor of a defendant's choice of counsel. It appears they were not.

DISSENT: (Stevens, J.) The Court gives insufficient weight to the informed and voluntary nature of Wheat's (D) waiver.

▌ ANALYSIS

The Sixth Amendment guarantees the right to counsel, but it is not absolute. It appears that the only certain right a defendant has regarding choice of representation is the right to waive counsel and represent himself, if he so chooses. This right was announced in *Faretta v. California*, 422 U.S. 806 (1975).

Quicknotes

CONFLICT OF INTEREST Refers to ethical problems that arise, or may be anticipated to arise, between an attorney and his client if the interests of the attorney, another client or a third party conflict with those of the present client.

SUBSTITUTION OF COUNSEL Refers to a situation in which a party seeks to terminate representation by a particular attorney or an attorney seeks to withdraw from a case; in order to substitute attorneys the party or attorney must obtain the court's permission, which may be denied if such substitution would result in an unfair delay or disruption of the proceedings.

Young v. United States ex rel. Vuitton et Fils S.A.

Infringer of trademark (D) v. Manufacturer of leather goods (P)

481 U.S. 787 (1987).

NATURE OF CASE: Review of criminal contempt citation.

FACT SUMMARY: In a criminal contempt proceeding ancillary to a trademark infringement suit, counsel for Vuitton et Fils S.A. (P) was appointed as prosecutor against Young (D).

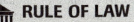 **RULE OF LAW**
Counsel for a party that is a beneficiary of a court order may not be appointed as a prosecutor in a contempt action alleging a violation of order.

FACTS: Vuitton et Fils S.A. (Vuitton) (P) filed a trademark infringement action against, among others, Young (D). Vuitton (P) obtained an injunction. After Young (D) violated the injunction, Vuitton (P) brought an action to show cause why Young (D) should not be held in contempt. Counsel for Vuitton (P) was appointed special prosecutor. Young (D) was convicted, and the Second Circuit Court of Appeals confirmed.

ISSUE: May counsel for a party that is the beneficiary of a court order be appointed as prosecutor in a contempt action alleging violation of that order?

HOLDING AND DECISION: (Brennan, J.) No. Counsel for a party that is the beneficiary of a court order may not be appointed as prosecutor in a contempt action alleging a violation of that order. The role of the criminal prosecutor is not to convict, but to seek justice. For that reason, prosecutors are forbidden by both federal law and professional ethics from representing the government in which they, their family, or their business associates have an interest. This Court has consistently applied to criminal contempt proceedings the same standards applicable to criminal prosecutions in general, and believes this prohibition to be applicable to such proceedings. Therefore, a prosecutor in a criminal contempt matter cannot have an interest in the order upon which the contempt is based. Here, counsel for Vuitton (P), the beneficiary of the allegedly violated order, was appointed prosecutor. Vuitton (P) plainly had an interest in seeing the order enforced. Counsel was therefore placed in a position of serving two masters, justice and Vuitton (P). This was improper and mandates a new trial. Reversed.

▶ **ANALYSIS**

The role of the prosecutor is described in various places in the law. A notable example is EC 7-13 of the ABA Model Code of Professional Responsibility. Per this section, prosecutors are ethically bound not to prosecute unless they are convinced of guilt.

Quicknotes

18 U.S.C. § 208(A) Federal prosecutors are prohibited from representing the government in any matter in which they, their family, or their business associates have any interest.

People v. Adams

State (P) v. Alleged harasser (D)

N.Y. Ct. App., 987 N.E.2d 272 (2013).

NATURE OF CASE: Appeal from denial of motion to disqualify the district attorney's office as prosecutor.

FACT SUMMARY: Adams's (D) defense counsel filed a motion to disqualify the district attorney's office as prosecutor of charges against Adams (D) because of an alleged conflict of interest. The complainant was a sitting city court judge and the district attorney's office, which appeared nearly daily in front of the judge, appeared to be handling Adams's (D) prosecution differently because of the complainant's status.

🏛 RULE OF LAW
Appearance of impropriety can be grounds for disqualification although the appearance must be of significance, and disqualification as a consequence is rare.

FACTS: Complainant, a sitting Rochester City Court judge, accused her neighbor and ex-paramour, Adams (D), of sending three vulgar, hostile text messages on her mobile phone. The messages had nothing to do with her status as a judge. Defendant was charged in Rochester City Court with two misdemeanor counts of aggravated harassment in the second degree. Assigned defense counsel withdrew and counsel from another county was appointed for Adams (D). Defense counsel spoke with the district attorney's office about a plea agreement, but the prosecutor stated the agreement, while fair, would not be offered because of the "position of the victim." Complainant insisted on going to trial. Adams's (D) counsel filed a motion to disqualify the district attorney's office on the basis of conflict of interest because the prosecutors regularly appeared before the judge and handled the proposed plea differently from every other similar case. [County Court denied the motion; Adams (D) appealed.]

ISSUE: Can the appearance of impropriety be grounds for disqualification?

HOLDING AND DECISION: (Pigott, J.) Yes. The appearance of impropriety can be grounds for disqualification although the appearance must be of significance, and disqualification as a consequence is rare. Adams's (D) motion to disqualify the district attorney's office included an affidavit from original defense counsel stating the district attorney's office was handling this matter differently than any other similar prosecution solely because of the status of the complainant. Affiant argued the district attorney was forced to behave differently to avoid hostility from the judge before whom prosecutors appeared nearly daily. A similarly situated defendant should have received an adjournment in contemplation of dismissal (ACD) or violation with an Order of Protection. In response to the motion, the district attorney's office generally denied the conflict of interest allegation but did not provide an example of other cases in which it refused to offer a plea nor did it specifically rebut the allegation it consistently accepted pleas to reduced charges in similar cases. While rare, the appearance of impropriety can be grounds for disqualification. The appearance would have to be so great that public trust in the government and rule of law might be eroded. Here, it does not appear the prosecutor is reviewing the case based on its merits or legitimate prosecutorial concerns. There is no right to a plea agreement, but the appearance is that the prosecutor is refusing to offer a plea because the complainant is a sitting judge. The alleged crimes were not related to her judicial position nor were the charges that unusual for a harassment case. Nonetheless, despite prolonged negotiations, the district attorney's office did not offer reduced charges or agree to a plea. Former defense counsel stated he had never seen prosecutors take such a stance in similar cases and the district attorney's office did not respond to the disqualification motion with anything more than conclusory denials. This case involves a significant appearance of impropriety, which requires disqualification. Reversed and remitted for further proceedings in accordance with this opinion.

▶ ANALYSIS

Defendants do not have a legal right to reduced charges or a plea offer, but the public must be able to rely on prosecutorial fairness in evaluating similarly situated cases. Adams (D) did not prove the existence of a conflict of interest, but the evidence supported the significant appearance of a conflict of interest. Perhaps the prosecutors were not taking the judge's status into consideration, but it is better to remove even the scintilla of doubt so the public can be assured justice is blind.

Quicknotes

DISQUALIFICATION A determination of unfitness or ineligibility.

Fiandaca v. Cunningham

Female prison inmates (P) v. State (D)

827 F.2d 825 (1st Cir. 1987).

NATURE OF CASE: Appeal of injunction issued in action based on alleged equal protection violation.

FACT SUMMARY: A settlement offer made by the state of New Hampshire (D) to a class of plaintiffs was contrary to the interest of another client of the offeree's attorney.

🏛 RULE OF LAW
An attorney may not represent two clients when a settlement offer made to one is contrary to the interests of the other.

FACTS: A class of plaintiffs comprised of female inmates of the New Hampshire (D) penitentiary system brought action in which they claimed that they were denied equal protection because male inmates enjoyed superior facilities. They were represented by New Hampshire Legal Assistance (NHLA), a public-interest legal organization. NHLA also represented a class of students at a state school in an unrelated matter. At one point the state (D) offered to convert one of the school buildings into a penitentiary for women. The students represented by NHLA vehemently opposed this, and the convict plaintiffs rejected the offer. A trial ensued, and the district court held that the state penitentiary system denied equal protection to female convicts and ordered that a facility be built. The state (D) appealed, contending that the court should have disqualified NHLA from representing the plaintiff class.

ISSUE: May an attorney represent two clients when a settlement offer made to one is contrary to the interest of the other?

HOLDING AND DECISION: (Coffin, J.) No. An attorney may not represent two clients when a settlement offer made to one is contrary to the interests of the other. Rule 1.7 of New Hampshire's Rules of Professional Conduct prohibits an attorney from representing a client if the representation of that client may be materially limited by the lawyer's responsibilities to another client. Loyalty to a client is materially limited when a lawyer cannot recommend a possible course of action due to loyalty to another client. Thus, when a settlement offer is made and a lawyer owes allegiance to a party opposed to that settlement, that lawyer cannot use his independent judgment in advising the client. At this point a conflict exists. Here, NHLA could not recommend the state's (D) settlement offer because of a duty to another client, and it therefore should have been disqualified. [The court went on to affirm the finding of an equal protection violation, holding it not to have been

tainted by the conflict, but ordered a retrial as to the remedy.] Vacated and remanded for a new trial.

▶ ANALYSIS

It is usually possible for a potential conflict to be waived. This requires (1) a reasonable belief by the attorney that he can zealously represent both interests, and (2) a knowing consent by the affected parties. The court here, however, believed the conflict to be real, not potential.

■■■

Quicknotes

CLASS ACTION A suit commenced by a representative on behalf of an ascertainable group that is too large to appear in court, who shares a commonality of interests and who will benefit from a successful result.

CONFLICT OF INTEREST Refers to ethical problems that arise, or may be anticipated to arise, between an attorney and his client if the interests of the attorney, another client or a third party conflict with those of the present client.

■■■

Simpson v. James

Restaurant owner (P) v. Attorney (D)

903 F.2d 372 (5th Cir. 1990).

NATURE OF CASE: Appeal of award of damages for professional malpractice.

FACT SUMMARY: Simpson (P), who retained Oliver (D) to represent her legally during the sale of her business, alleged that Oliver (D) committed malpractice by representing the buyers of her business as well.

🏛 RULE OF LAW
An attorney may commit malpractice by representing both sides in a transaction.

FACTS: Simpson (P) operated a restaurant, which she desired to sell. She contacted James (D), an attorney who had previously represented her, concerning a sale. Oliver (D), James's (D) partner, facilitated a transaction between Simpson (P) and Tide Creek, Inc. A deal was arranged wherein the business was sold for $500,000, $100,000 of which was paid down, with $400,000 payable in notes, secured by Tide Creek stock. The business proved unprofitable for Tide Creek, which eventually went bankrupt. Simpson (P) sued Oliver (D) and James (D), who had represented both sides in the transaction, contending that it had constituted malpractice for them to do so. A jury awarded Simpson (P) $200,000, and an appeal was made.

ISSUE: May an attorney commit malpractice by representing both sides in a transaction?

HOLDING AND DECISION: (Wisdom, J.) Yes. An attorney may commit malpractice by representing both sides in a transaction. While representing both sides is not inherently impermissible, it may make it difficult for an attorney to represent one side, the other, or both as zealously as professional standards require. Here, the jury found that James's (D) and Oliver's (D) failure to adequately safeguard Simpson's (P) pecuniary interests, such as creating a lien on Tide Creek's stock rather than the business's assets, proximately harmed Simpson (P). This was a permissible finding for the jury. Affirmed.

▶ ANALYSIS

Upon examination, it can be concluded that dual representation didn't really figure into the result here, at least not directly. The malpractice was not a conflict of interest, although the conflict might have caused the behavior that constituted the malpractice. It would seem that an attorney who didn't represent the buyers would have been equally liable had he acted as did the defendants here. The facts given in the opinion do not shed light on whether the attorney would have acted differently absent the dual representation, so it is impossible to say whether the dual representation led to the malpractice.

Quicknotes

CONFLICT OF INTEREST Refers to ethical problems that arise, or may be anticipated to arise, between an attorney and his client if the interests of the attorney, another client or a third party conflict with those of the present client.

NEGLIGENCE Conduct falling below the standard of care that a reasonable person would demonstrate under similar conditions.

Public Service Mutual Insurance Co. v. Goldfarb

Insurance company (P) v. Dentist (D)

N.Y. Ct. App., 53 N.Y.2d 392, 425 N.E.2d 810 (1981).

NATURE OF CASE: Action for declaratory judgment of insurance noncoverage.

FACT SUMMARY: Public Service Mutual Insurance Co. (P) contended that Goldfarb's (D) acts of sexual assault on a dental patient did not trigger a duty to defend and indemnify him in a civil suit.

🏛 RULE OF LAW
Sexual assault by a doctor against a patient may trigger a professional liability carrier's duty to defend and indemnify in a subsequent civil suit.

FACTS: Goldfarb (D), a dentist, was accused by one of his patients of sexually assaulting her while she was under sedation. Criminal charges were filed, and Goldfarb (D) was convicted. The victim filed a civil suit against Goldfarb (D), which he tendered to his professional liability carrier, Public Service Mutual Insurance Co. (Public Service) (P). Public Service (P) responded by seeking a declaration that the alleged acts did not trigger a duty to defend and indemnify Goldfarb (D). [The casebook excerpt does not state the trial court or appellate division results.]

ISSUE: May sexual assault by a doctor against a patient trigger a duty to defend and indemnify in a subsequent civil suit?

HOLDING AND DECISION: (Jasen, J.) Yes. Sexual assault by a doctor against a patient may trigger a professional liability carrier's duty to defend and indemnify in a subsequent civil suit. To the extent that a jury in the civil suit finds that injury upon the victim was unintentionally caused, the duty to indemnify will arise. Since this determination cannot be made prior to trial, Public Service (P) must defend Goldfarb (D) for as long as the potential of a duty to indemnify exists, the duty to defend also exists. [The casebook excerpt does not state whether the present opinion constituted a reversal, affirmation, or modification.]

▶ ANALYSIS

The reasoning used in arriving at the rule here is fairly universal. The duty to defend arises when any aspect of an action might be covered. The terminology used is "the duty to defend is broader than the duty to indemnify." The most influential case in this area is *Gray v. Zurich Ins. Co.*, 65 Cal. 2d 263 (1966), the first case to clearly delineate the broadness of the duty to defend.

Quicknotes

COMPENSATORY DAMAGES Measure of damages necessary to compensate victim for actual injuries suffered.

INDEMNIFICATION The payment by a corporation of expenses incurred by its officers or directors as a result of litigation involving the corporation.

PUNITIVE DAMAGES Damages exceeding the actual injury suffered for the purposes of punishment, deterrence and comfort to plaintiff.

Successive Conflicts of Interest

Quick Reference Rules of Law

Analytica, Inc. v. NPD Research, Inc.

Competing company (P) v. Research company (D)

708 F.2d 1263 (7th Cir. 1983).

NATURE OF CASE: Appeal of order disqualifying counsel.

FACT SUMMARY: The same law firm that once represented NPD Research, Inc. (NPD) (D) represented a former principal of NPD in a subsequent suit against it.

RULE OF LAW
A law firm may not represent a principal of a former client in a lawsuit against the former client.

FACTS: Malec was an employee of NPD Research, Inc. (NPD) (D), who was given an equity interest as compensation for certain services. The law firm of Schwartz & Freeman handled the transaction. Subsequent to this Malec left NPD (D), forming Analytica, Inc. (P), which established itself as a competitor of NPD in market research. Analytica (P) subsequently filed an antitrust action against NPD (D). Analytica (P) was represented by Schwartz & Freeman. NPD (D) moved to disqualify Schwartz & Freeman. The district court granted the motion, and Analytica (P) appealed.

ISSUE: May a law firm represent a principal of its former client in a lawsuit against the former client?

HOLDING AND DECISION: (Posner, J.) No. A law firm may not represent a principal of its former client in a lawsuit against the former client. Specifically, a lawyer may not represent an adversary of his former client if the subject matter of the two representations is substantially related. If confidential information that might have been obtained during a representation might be relevant in the second, then the attorney must be disqualified. The fact that the attorney might not have actually attained the information is of no consequence. A per se rule of disqualification is preferable, as determination of the facts underlying a motion to disqualify would be difficult and time consuming if a case-by-case analysis were employed. Here, Schwartz & Freeman represented NPD (D) in a financial transaction, and then represented an adversary in an antitrust suit. It seems clear that information that the firm might have obtained during its representation of NPD (D) might be relevant in the present action, so disqualification was proper. Affirmed.

▍ANALYSIS

The rule stated here is universal. In the current age of megafirms, it sometimes presents a problem in that disqualification of one member of a firm usually disqualifies the entire firm. A large firm might have many clients and the possibilities of inadvertent conflicts are ever present.

■━■

Quicknotes

CONFLICT OF INTEREST Refers to ethical problems that arise, or may be anticipated to arise, between an attorney and his client if the interests of the attorney, another client or a third party conflict with those of the present client.

■━■

Cromley v. Board of Education

Teacher (P) v. School (D)

17 F.3d 1059 (7th Cir.), *cert. denied*, 513 U.S. 816 (1994).

NATURE OF CASE: Appeal from judgment granting defendant's motion for summary judgment and denying plaintiff's motion to disqualify defendants' attorneys in 42 U.S.C. § 1983 action.

FACT SUMMARY: During Cromley's (P) suit against the Board of Education (the Board) (D), her attorney, Weiner, withdrew from the case after accepting a partnership in the law firm representing the Board (D), but the district court denied Cromley's (P) motion to disqualify the Board's (D) attorneys.

> 🏛 **RULE OF LAW**
> When a lawyer in a case moves to the other party's law firm, the attorneys for the other party must be disqualified where the representations are substantially related, unless the presumption of shared confidences can be rebutted.

FACTS: Cromley (P), a high school teacher, brought an action under 42 U.S.C. § 1983 against the Board of Education (the Board) (D), claiming she had been denied various administrative positions because she had complained to a state agency about the sexual misconduct of a co-worker. During extended pretrial litigation, Cromley's (P) attorney, Weiner, accepted a partnership in the law firm representing the Board (D). Weiner then withdrew as Cromley's (P) attorney. The district court granted summary judgment to the Board (D), denying Cromley's (P) motion to disqualify the Board's (D) attorneys. Cromley (P) appealed.

ISSUE: When a lawyer in a case moves to the other party's law firm, must the attorneys for the other party be disqualified where the representations are substantially related, unless the presumption of shared confidences can be rebutted?

HOLDING AND DECISION: (Ripple, J.) Yes. When a lawyer in a case moves to the other party's law firm, the attorneys for the other party must be disqualified where the representations are substantially related, unless the presumption of shared confidences can be rebutted. The subject matter both before and after Weiner changed law firms was Cromley's (P) lawsuit against the Board (D). However, in this case, the presumption of shared confidences has been successfully rebutted by the timely establishment of a screening process. After he joined the Board's (D) law firm, Weiner was denied access to the relevant files. Under threat of discipline, he and all employees of the firm were admonished not to discuss the case. In addition, Weiner was not allowed to share in the fees derived from the case. The partner handling the case for

the Board (D) affirmed under oath that all the admonitions have been adhered to. Affirmed.

▶ **ANALYSIS**

Other factors help to determine whether adequate protection of the former client's confidences has been achieved. Those factors include the size of the law firm, its structural divisions, the screened attorney's position in the firm, the likelihood of contact between the screened attorney and one representing another party, and the fact that a law firm's and lawyer's most valuable asset are their reputations for honesty, integrity, and competence. The presumption of shared confidences has been found to be irrebuttable only when an entire law firm changes sides.

Quicknotes

CONFLICT OF INTEREST Refers to ethical problems that arise, or may be anticipated to arise, between an attorney and his client if the interests of the attorney, another client or a third party conflict with those of the present client.

Armstrong v. McAlpin

Receiver (P) v. Alleged thieves (D)

625 F.2d 433 (2d Cir. 1980) (en banc), *vacated on other grounds*, 449 U.S. 1106 (1981).

NATURE OF CASE: Appeal of denial of motion to disqualify attorney of record.

FACT SUMMARY: Altman, an attorney who had been involved in a Securities and Exchange Commission investigation against McAlpin (D), later joined the firm representing the receiver appointed to recover allegedly stolen funds, which McAlpin (D) contended constituted a conflict.

⬛ RULE OF LAW
It is not a per se ground for disqualification when an attorney involved in a government investigation joins a private firm involved in litigation concerning the same matter.

FACTS: The Securities and Exchange Commission (SEC) commenced an investigation against McAlpin (D) and others, believing them to have looted the company they controlled. A receiver was eventually appointed to attempt to recover the company's funds. The firm of Gordon Hurwitz was retained by Armstrong (P), the receiver. Altman, who had been an attorney with the SEC and was involved in the original probe, was now a new attorney at Gordon Hurwitz. McAlpin (D) moved to disqualify Gordon Hurwitz, contending that the presence of Altman constituted a conflict. The district court, after receiving testimony that Altman was screened from ongoing litigation, denied the motion. A Second Circuit Court of Appeals panel reversed, holding that government service per se disqualifies a firm that included a former government attorney from handling an action in which the attorney had previously been involved. The Second Circuit held a rehearing en banc.

ISSUE: Is it a per se ground for disqualification when an attorney involved in a government investigation joins a private firm involved in litigation concerning the same matter?

HOLDING AND DECISION: (Feinberg, J.) No. It is not a per se ground for disqualification when an attorney involved in a government investigation joins a private firm involved in litigation concerning the same matter. Under DR 5-105(D) of the ABA Code of Professional Responsibility, the disqualification of one firm member disqualifies the entire firm. However, policy reasons exist for not applying this rule when the cause of the conflict is prior government service. If it were applied, it would be extremely difficult for the government to obtain qualified lawyers to work for it, as they would face the prospect of being unable to obtain private employment

ever again. Rather, the better review is to consider disqualification on a case-by-case basis. If a court finds the prior government attorney to be effectively screened from the private litigation, disqualification is not necessary. Here, that was the holding of the district court, and it was a proper ruling. Panel opinion vacated; district court affirmed. [On a petition for certiorari, the United States Supreme Court held the order nonappealable, and vacated both the panel and the en banc options.]

▶ ANALYSIS

Due to the proliferation of both government and large, multi-state law firms, the problem addressed here has become more common in recent years. The solution reached by the district court, accepting a screening of the disqualified attorney from the litigation in question, has been the most common response. While technically a violation of DR 5-105(D), this "Chinese wall" approach has been accepted in many jurisdictions.

━━━■■■■■■━━━

Quicknotes

DISQUALIFICATION A determination of unfitness or ineligibility.

Ethics in Advocacy

Quick Reference Rules of Law

Nix v. Whiteside

Unidentified (P) v. Convicted killer (D)

475 U.S. 157 (1986).

NATURE OF CASE: Review of order granting habeas corpus subsequent to murder conviction.

FACT SUMMARY: Whiteside (D) contended that his counsel's refusal to allow him to commit perjury denied him his right to counsel.

🏛 RULE OF LAW
A criminal defendant is not denied his right to counsel if his counsel refuses to allow him to commit perjury.

FACTS: An altercation involving Whiteside (D) resulted in the stabbing death of another. Prior to testifying, Whiteside (D) told his attorney that he intended to state that he had seen a gun in the decedent's hand, even though he had previously stated to the contrary. The attorney informed him that to do so would constitute perjury, which he could not allow. The attorney informed Whiteside (D) that if he did so testify, he would inform the court of Whiteside's (D) perjury. Whiteside (D) did not so testify, and he was convicted of murder. He appealed, contending that counsel's threats to expose his perjury constituted a denial of counsel under the Sixth Amendment. This conviction was affirmed. Whiteside (D) petitioned for habeas corpus in district court. This was denied. The court of appeals reversed, agreeing with Whiteside's (D) contention. The United States Supreme Court granted review.

ISSUE: Is a criminal defendant denied his right to counsel if his counsel refuses to allow him to commit perjury?

HOLDING AND DECISION: (Burger, C.J.) No. A criminal defendant is not denied his right to counsel if his counsel refuses to allow him to commit perjury. The Sixth Amendment's right to counsel clause is not abridged unless counsel is so ineffective as to not have been functioning as counsel. It is the duty of the counsel to take all lawful measures to exonerate his client. However, counsel has no right to violate the law, or to assist others in doing so. Further, DR 7-102 of the ABA Code of Professional Responsibility prohibits an attorney from knowingly using perjured testimony or false evidence. Since counsel is not permitted to assist in perjury, it can hardly be considered ineffectiveness when he refuses to do so. Here, the only basis for Whiteside's (D) contention regarding ineffectiveness was the refusal to allow him to perjure himself, and therefore no Sixth Amendment violation occurred. Reversed.

CONCURRENCE: (Brennan, J.) The Court can neither set rules of ethical conduct for lawyers practicing in the state courts nor enjoy statutory grants of jurisdiction over legal ethics.

CONCURRENCE: (Blackmun, J.) Whiteside's (D) argument is that he would have been acquitted had he been allowed to testify falsely. The answer to this is that the prevention of perjury can never be the basis for a conclusion that the trial was unfair, and therefore a defendant can never claim prejudice due to such prevention.

CONCURRENCE: (Stevens, J.) It should be remembered that recollections can and do augment themselves upon reflection, and the question is open as to how counsel should behave if it is not clear, as it was here, that perjury was in the offing.

▶ ANALYSIS

It has never been affirmatively held that an accused has an absolute right to testify on his behalf. In fact, at one time an accused was categorically prohibited from such testimony. While not expressly approving such a right, the Court here simply noted in passing that such a right is universally recognized.

■■■

Quicknotes

PERJURY The making of false statements under oath.

■■■

People v. Marshall

State (P) v. Accused murderer (D)

Ill. App. Ct., 995 N.E.2d 1045 (2013).

NATURE OF CASE: Appeal from murder conviction.

FACT SUMMARY: The prosecutor used racially charged language throughout Marshall's (D) trial for murder when race played no role in the offense.

🏛 RULE OF LAW
Prosecution's demonstration of egregious racial prejudice during trial denies defendant the right to a fair trial.

FACTS: Lacy and Blye provided statements to the police, recanted those statements, and then testified on behalf of the government (P) during Marshall's (D) murder trial. The prosecutor (P) sought to explain the change in their story from the time of their statements to the time of testifying. In his opening statement, the prosecutor (P) repeatedly referenced the "black culture" in Marion. He distinguished "people like us" who trust the police from the distrust of the police by the "black community in Marion." He continued referencing race and the difference in trust in law enforcement throughout the trial. The jury convicted Marshall (D). [Marshall (D) appealed.]

ISSUE: Does prosecution's demonstration of egregious racial prejudice during trial deny defendant the right to a fair trial?

HOLDING AND DECISION: (Goldenhersh, J.) Yes. Prosecution's demonstration of egregious racial prejudice during trial denies defendant the right to a fair trial. The prosecutor informed the jury their understanding of the black culture in Marion would decide the witnesses's credibility and "most of the other issues in this case." The Court cannot say the jury did not consider such inflammatory remarks when reaching the verdict. A prosecutor may argue fair and reasonable inferences from the evidence adduced at trial during his closing argument, but no evidence of the racial makeup of Marion was introduced during trial. The "facts" he used during his closing argument had no basis and were naked prejudice. Finally, the prosecutor improperly aligned himself with the jury when he contrasted the "black community" with "our white world." References to race have been found to be plain error. These errors were substantial. Reversed and remanded.

▶ ANALYSIS

A prosecutor may help a jury understand the import of certain evidence introduced at trial. The prosecutor cannot play on a jury's assumed prejudices as a basis for conviction. A closing argument may be colorful, but it must be based on facts found during the trial.

━━■■■━━

Quicknotes

PREJUDICE A preference of the court towards one party prior to litigation.

━━■■■━━

Zapata v. Vasquez

Alleged murderer (D) v. [Party not identified.] (P)

788 F.3d 1106 (9th Cir. 2015).

NATURE OF CASE: Appeal from denial of claim of ineffective assistance of counsel at trial.

FACT SUMMARY: At Zapata's (D) criminal trial, the prosecutor concocted a story for summation about Trigueros's last minutes, including Zapata (D) shouting ethnic slurs at Trigueros. The evidence did not support the prosecutor's story, but the judge and the defense counsel permitted the prosecutor to weave the tale for the jury just prior to deliberation. The jury convicted Zapata (D) of charges for the first-degree murder of Trigueros.

🏛 RULE OF LAW
Closing arguments unsupported by evidence and designed to elicit a decision based on emotion rather than evidence may constitute prejudice.

FACTS: Trigueros, a 19-year-old student, was fatally shot in what appeared to be a gang-related shooting although no evidence suggested Trigueros was a member of the rival gang of Zapata (D), the alleged murderer. At Zapata's (D) trial, prosecutor Scott presented his closing rebuttal argument to the jury. Scott wove an emotional and completely fabricated tale about Trigueros's last minutes during which an angry Zapata (D) yelled ethnic slurs at the frightened, confused victim. None of the evidence remotely suggested any of this was true. Zapata's (D) defense counsel did not object to the story or the ethnic slurs attributed to his client. The judge did not instruct the jury about the false tale. The jury convicted Zapata (D) of first-degree murder. [Zapata (D) appealed his conviction to the California Court of Appeals based on ineffective assistance of counsel; the appeal was denied; Zapata (D) appealed.]

ISSUE: May closing arguments unsupported by evidence and designed to elicit a decision based on emotion rather than evidence constitute prejudice?

HOLDING AND DECISION: (Fisher, J.) Yes. Closing arguments unsupported by evidence and designed to elicit a decision based on emotion rather than evidence may constitute prejudice. Here, the prosecutor presented to the jury a fabricated and emotional story of Trigueros's last minutes as if it was true. The only eyewitness to the murder testified he could not hear what Zapata (D) was yelling. Zapata's (D) extensive gang-related criminal history was presented at trial and Scott, the prosecutor, deliberately blurred the lines between Zapata's (D) past convictions and the current crime. The story also included specific ethnic slurs designed to inflame the jury's passions. This increases the risk the jury convicted on emotion rather than evidence. This case also differs from others in which prosecutorial misconduct existed because, here, the misconduct was prejudicial. The statements were "pure fiction," no evidence suggested that these slurs used in prior Zapata (D) incidents were used here, and neither the defense counsel nor the judge tempered the prosecutor's fictional story. The defense counsel provided ineffective assistance of counsel when he failed to object to the false tale and inflammatory epithets told to the jury minutes prior to its deliberation. Reversed and remanded.

▶ ANALYSIS

Closing arguments are meant to be persuasive and frequently are the attorney's best chance to tell the story of the case to the jury. The summation, however, must be based on the evidence presented during the trial. The fact-finders and the clients rely on counsel to argue persuasively and effectively without veering into the false and the inflammatory. A skilled attorney can package compellingly the facts and evidence actually presented in a case without resorting to complete fiction.

Quicknotes

INEFFECTIVE ASSISTANCE OF COUNSEL A claim brought by an accused in which it must be determined whether the attorney's rendering of representation was such that the ultimate disposition of the case may not be relied upon as fair.

Mullaney v. Aude

Ex-boyfriend (D) v. Ex-girlfriend (P)

Md. Ct. Spec. App., 126 Md. App. 639, 730 A.2d 759 (1999).

NATURE OF CASE: Appeal from imposition of attorneys' fees.

FACT SUMMARY: Mullaney's (D) lawyer, Mr. Harris, insulted both Ms. Aude (P) and Ms. Green, her attorney, by making gender-biased remarks and insinuations during a deposition in front of other attorneys.

🏛 RULE OF LAW
A lawyer may not use gender-biased tactics to gain advantage during the course of the litigation process.

FACTS: One of the defendant's lawyers, Mr. Harris, made a derogatory comment to the plaintiff during the course of a deposition. When Ms. Green, one of the plaintiff's lawyers, told Mr. Harris that his remark was in poor taste and asked him to refrain from making any further derogatory statements, Mr. Harris insulted Ms. Green by making nasty insinuations and further referring to Ms. Green as "babe."

ISSUE: May a court properly impose attorneys' fees as a sanction for using gender bias in the litigation process to gain an advantage over an adversary?

HOLDING AND DECISION: (Adkins, J.) Yes. Courts have a duty to require the attorneys who practice before them to conduct themselves in a professional manner. That includes refraining from behavior and statements that are biased or prejudiced based on race, sex, religion, national origin, disability, age, sexual orientation, or socio-economic status. The court makes clear that the use of gender-bias tactics to evoke an emotional reaction in an adversary will not be tolerated. Affirmed.

▶ ANALYSIS

This case is one of many clearly calling for a return to civility. Judges do not indulge this and other types of less blatant behavior and often impose sanctions and other forms of discipline. Foul language and name calling are other forms of intimidation that are not permitted.

━━━

Quicknotes

DEPOSITION A pretrial discovery procedure whereby oral or written questions are asked by one party of the opposing party or of a witness for the opposing party under oath in preparation for litigation.

━━━

Thul v. OneWest Bank, FSB

[Party not identified.] (P) v. Banking institution (D)

2013 WL 212926 (N.D. Ill. 2013).

NATURE OF CASE: Court's order to show cause on sanctions against counsel.

FACT SUMMARY: Counsel for OneWest Bank, FSB failed to cite adverse precedent in their brief supporting their motion to dismiss Thul's (P) petition.

🏛 RULE OF LAW
Counsel is obligated to bring known adverse precedent to the court's attention.

FACTS: Three attorneys from Skadden, Arps, Meagher & Flom represented OneWest Bank, FSB (OneWest) (D). On behalf of their client, they moved to dismiss Thul's (P) petition. Counsel filed a brief in support of the motion and Thul's (P) counsel filed a brief in response. *Wigod v. Wells Fargo Bank, N.S.*, 673 F.3d 547 (7th Cir. 2012), was precedent directly adverse to OneWest's (D) position, but OneWest's (D) counsel failed to cite it in its brief. The court issued its order to show cause why counsel should not be sanctioned for its failure to cite the adverse case.

ISSUE: Is counsel obligated to bring known adverse precedent to the court's attention?

HOLDING AND DECISION: (Kennelly, J.) Yes. Counsel is obligated to bring known adverse precedent to the court's attention. Here, one of the attorneys was an associate who personally had no knowledge of *Wigod* and relied on the briefing of the other two senior attorneys. The motion to show cause is vacated against him. The other two attorneys admitted their knowledge of *Wigod* and their failure to include it in their brief. They contend it is factually distinguishable, so they believed it did not need to be included. The court disagrees. The two, however, sincerely apologized to the court and to opposing counsel. Their firm has contributed financially to the interim settlement as a means of redressing Thul's (P) counsel expenses related to responding to the motion to dismiss. Also, the attorneys are named in the order to show cause, this order, and they were orally admonished during the hearing. The court will impose no further sanction. [Decision not stated in casebook excerpt.]

▌ ANALYSIS

It is not the job of opposing counsel to inform the court of adverse cases to a client's position. Each attorney has the affirmative obligation to inform the court of known adverse precedent. The attorney then can factually distinguish the case or argue why that law should be inapplicable in the present case. Failure to direct the court to all relevant cases, even ones that adversely impact one's client, can result in sanctions and ethics charges.

■■■

Quicknotes

SHOW CAUSE Generally referred to as an order to show cause or a show cause order. The order is directed to the opposing party to appear and show cause why a certain order should not be enforced or confirmed, or give reason why a court should take or not take a proposed action.

■■■

Special Issues in Criminal Prosecutions

Quick Reference Rules of Law

In re Ryder

N/A

263 F. Supp. 360 (E.D. Va. 1967).

NATURE OF CASE: Court's own motion to suspend attorney from practice for criminal misconduct.

FACTS SUMMARY: Ryder, an attorney, hid stolen money and a sawed-off shotgun belonging to his client in a safe-deposit box at his bank with the intention of keeping it there until after his client's trial for armed robbery.

> **🏛 RULE OF LAW**
> A defense attorney's withholding of incriminating evidence during a criminal proceeding for the purpose of hindering the preparation of the prosecution's case constitutes unethical deception and misconduct.

FACTS: Cook robbed a bank at gunpoint and deposited the proceeds as well as his sawed-off shotgun in a bank safe-deposit box. Some of the cash Cook obtained was "bait money," the serial numbers of which had been recorded. During an interview with the FBI, Cook turned over some of this "bait money," but called Ryder, an attorney who had represented him in a previous civil matter, and asked him to attend the interview. Ryder did and had the agents leave. Cook then insisted he had not robbed the bank and had obtained the money at a crap game. Ryder telephoned one of the FBI agents, who told him that the serial numbers of the money Cook turned over matched some of those taken from the bank. Ryder then again asked Cook about the robbery, but Cook replied that on the day of the robbery a man had offered him $500 to put a package in a safe-deposit box. Ryder then consulted with various attorneys and judges in confidence about whether it would be proper to have a third party obtain the money in Cook's box and what would constitute a proper course of conduct thereafter. The advice of these lawyers was mixed and ambiguous. Ryder then asked Cook to execute a power of attorney authorizing access to Cook's safe-deposit box and authorizing him to dispose of its contents "as he saw fit" and "in a way that wouldn't harm Cook." Cook did so. Ryder then went to the bank and transferred the contents of Cook's box, the stolen money and the sawed-off shotgun, to a box in his own name. Ryder did not intend to notify the prosecution about this evidence, but only intended to turn it over if the government learned of it independently. Cook was then indicted for armed robbery, and FBI agents with search warrants for both Cook's and Ryder's boxes found Cook's contraband and weapon. The local federal district court then removed Ryder as Cook's counsel, suspended him from practice, referred the matter to the local U.S.

Attorney, and set a hearing for further disciplinary proceedings against Ryder.

ISSUE: Does a defense attorney's withholding of incriminating evidence during a criminal proceeding for the purpose of hindering the preparation of the prosecutor's case constitute unethical deception and misconduct?

HOLDING AND DECISION: (Per curiam) Yes. A defense attorney's withholding of incriminating evidence during a criminal proceeding for the purpose of hindering the preparation of the prosecutor's case constitutes unethical deception and misconduct. Ryder took possession of the stolen money and sawed-off shotgun specifically to destroy the chain of evidence linking his client to the robbery. He intended to retain the evidence until at least after Cook's trial, unless the government first discovered it and compelled its production. Ryder knew that the money was stolen, that the man who robbed the bank used a sawed-off shotgun, that Cook's possession of the shotgun was illegal, and that his larceny was a continuing offense. He also knew that the laws against concealing stolen property and forbidding receipt and possession of a sawed-off shotgun contained no exemptions for lawyers. Thus, Ryder used the office of attorney in violation of the law in an effort to destroy an evidentiary presumption. Ryder would be disbarred were it not for two factors in mitigation: he intended to return the money after Cook's trial; and he consulted several attorneys before deciding on a course of conduct he may have believed constituted acting in the best interests of his client. [Ryder was ordered suspended from the practice of law for 18 months.]

▶ ANALYSIS

The holdings of other cases are in accord with this decision. See, e.g., *People v. Superior Court (Fairbank)*, 192 Cal. App. 3d 32, 237 Cal. Rptr. 158 (1987) (a criminal defense lawyer must inform the court that he has taken possession of stolen property at issue in the criminal proceeding, even if it cannot be shown that the prosecution "needs" the evidence to prepare its case). See also *Commonwealth v. Stenbach*, 356 Pa. Super. 5, 514 A.2d 114 (1986), leave to appeal denied 517 Pa. 589, 534 A.2d 769 (1987) (lawyers are under an ethical obligation to turn over physical evidence to opposing counsel or to the court). Cf. N.Y. State Bar Committee on Professional Ethics, Opinion No. 479 (Mar. 6, 1978) (attorney whose client was indicted for murder learned from the client the location of the bodies of victims of prior murders and actually took photographs

Continued on next page.

of the bodies; it was held that it was not improper for the attorney to fail to reveal the location of the bodies or to use this knowledge with his client's approval in plea bargaining).

Quicknotes

ATTORNEY-CLIENT PRIVILEGE A doctrine precluding the admission into evidence of confidential communications between an attorney and his client made in the course of obtaining professional assistance.

POWER OF ATTORNEY A written instrument that allows a person to appoint an agent and confer authority to perform certain specified acts on his behalf.

People v. Meredith

State (P) v. Convicted robber and murderer (D)

Cal. Sup. Ct., 29 Cal. 3d 682, 631 P.2d 46 (1981).

NATURE OF CASE: Appeal of conviction of robbery and murder.

FACT SUMMARY: An investigator working for criminal defendant Scott's (D) attorney observed and took possession of a wallet that had been taken from the victim and disposed of by Scott (D).

RULE OF LAW

The attorney-client privilege does not protect from disclosure testimony regarding observations made by counsel or his agent concerning evidence that has been removed by counsel or the agent.

FACTS: Meredith (D) was charged with the robbery and murder of one Wade. Also charged was Scott (D). Scott (D) told Schenk, his counsel, that after Meredith (D) had killed Wade, Scott (D) took Wade's wallet and disposed of it in a trash container near Scott's (D) home. Schenk dispatched Frick, an investigator, to retrieve the wallet. Frick found the wallet and brought it to Schenk, who eventually turned it over to the prosecution. At trial, Frick was subpoenaed to testify about where he had found the wallet. The testimony was admitted over Scott's (D) attorney-client privilege objection. Scott (D) was convicted, and the state court of appeals affirmed. The California Supreme Court granted review.

ISSUE: Does the attorney-client privilege protect from disclosure testimony regarding observations made by counsel or his agent concerning evidence that has been removed by counsel or agent?

HOLDING AND DECISION: (Tobriner, J.) No. The attorney-client privilege does not protect from disclosure testimony regarding observations made by counsel or his agent concerning evidence that has been removed by counsel or the agent. Deciding this issue requires the balancing of competing considerations. On the one hand, to deny protection to observations arising from confidential communications could chill protected attorney-client communication. On the other hand, the privilege cannot be extended so far as to render immune from discovery evidence first obtained by the defense. It cannot be doubted that communications between counsel and his investigator are protected by the privilege. From this it is not a large step to conclude information acquired solely as a result of such communications are also protected. Here, Frick's knowledge of the location of the wallet was a result of information obtained from Schenk, so without more, introduction of testimony regarding his observations would be protected. However, when counsel or his agent takes the extra step of moving or altering the evidence, the opportunity of the prosecution to observe it is forever lost. To hold that testimony regarding the original state of the evidence cannot be compelled under these circumstances would effectively permit the defense to destroy critical evidence, a result not contemplated by the attorney-client privilege. Here, Frick did in fact remove the wallet, so the prosecution was properly permitted to question him concerning it. Affirmed.

ANALYSIS

Both the law and the Code of Professional Responsibility place a duty on attorneys with respect to evidence. As to testimonial evidence, an attorney may not facilitate perjury. As to tangible evidence, an attorney may not falsify the same. The subject is covered in Disciplinary Rule 7-102(A).

■=■

Quicknotes

ATTORNEY-CLIENT PRIVILEGE A doctrine precluding the admission into evidence of confidential communications between an attorney and his client made in the course of obtaining professional assistance.

DUTY OF CANDOR/DUTY OF FAIRNESS Ethical duty to turn over an instrumentality of crime once it has been used to aid a client's case, owed to the tribunal and opposing counsel to prevent the frustration of justice.

■=■

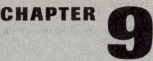

Negotiation and Transactional Matters

Quick Reference Rules of Law

Fire Insurance Exchange v. Bell

Insurance company (D) v. Injured claimant (P)

Ind. Sup. Ct., 643 N.E.2d 310 (1994).

NATURE OF CASE: Appeal from denial of motion for summary judgment.

FACT SUMMARY: Jason Bell (P), a claimant against Fire Insurance Exchange (D), an insurance company, argued that his attorney had the right to rely on the insurance company attorneys' intentional misrepresentations as to the company's policy limits.

🏛 RULE OF LAW
An attorney has the right to rely upon representations made by opposing counsel.

FACTS: Jason Bell (P), an infant, was severely burned by leaking gasoline at his grandfather's apartment. His guardian sued the insurer of the apartment. Robert Collins was retained to represent Bell (P) in his insurance claims. During negotiations, counsel for the insurance company intentionally made misrepresentations to Collins as to the limits of insurance coverage, stating the limits to be $100,000 when actually the limits were $300,000. Collins subsequently informed Bell (P) that he had been deceived intentionally by the opposing insurance counsel, whereupon Bell (P) brought suit against Fire Insurance Exchange (D), the insurer, for its attorneys' fraudulent misrepresentation of the policy limits. Fire Insurance Exchange (D) moved for summary judgment, arguing there was no right to rely on its attorneys' representations. The motion was denied, and Fire Insurance Exchange (D) appealed.

ISSUE: Does an attorney have the right to rely upon representations made by opposing counsel?

HOLDING AND DECISION: (Dickson, J.) Yes. An attorney has the right to rely upon representations made by opposing counsel. Courts have a particular constitutional responsibility with respect to the supervision of the practice of law. The reliability and trustworthiness of attorney representations constitute an important component of the efficient administration of justice. A lawyer's representations have long been accorded a particular expectation of honesty and trustworthiness. In this regard, the Indiana Oath of Attorneys includes the promise that a lawyer will employ such means only as are consistent with truth. Furthermore, the Indiana Professional Responsibility Rules declare that it is professional misconduct for a lawyer to engage in conduct involving dishonesty, fraud, deceit, or misrepresentation. Numerous other sources of guidelines and standards for lawyer conduct emphasize this basic principle. This court, accordingly, rejects the argument that plaintiff's counsel had no right to rely on the representations he claims because he had the means to ascertain

the relevant facts, was sophisticated, was in an adverse position, and that accurate policy limits information could have been obtained through formal discovery. This court declines to require attorneys to burden unnecessarily the courts and litigation process with discovery to verify the truthfulness of material representations made by opposing counsel. The law should promote lawyers' care in making statements that are accurate and trustworthy and should foster the reliance upon such statements by others. Affirmed.

▶ ANALYSIS

As emphasized in the *Bell* decision, in fulfilling the duty to represent a client vigorously, lawyers need be mindful of their obligation to the administration of justice, which is a truth-seeking process designed to resolve human and societal problems in a rational, peaceful, and efficient manner.

◼▬◼

Quicknotes

ATTORNEY-CLIENT PRIVILEGE A doctrine precluding the admission into evidence of confidential communications between an attorney and his client made in the course of obtaining professional assistance.

◼▬◼

Hoyt Properties, Inc. v. Production Resource Group, L.L.C.

Landlord (P) v. Tenant (D)

Minn. Sup. Ct., 736 N.W.2d 313 (2007).

NATURE OF CASE: Appeal from reversal of a summary judgment dismissal of an action to invalidate a settlement agreement.

FACT SUMMARY: Production Resource Group, L.L.C. (PRG) (D) contended that a statement made by its attorney to Hoyt Properties, Inc. (Hoyt) (P) that there was no basis for piercing the corporate veil of its subsidiary, Entolo, to reach PRG (D) was not a fraudulent misrepresentation of fact but a legal opinion, and that, therefore, a release agreement reached between Hoyt (P) and PRG (D) should not be rescinded on the basis of PRG's (D) attorney's statement to Hoyt (P).

🏛 RULE OF LAW
(1) A statement made by an attorney is actionable as a fraudulent misrepresentation where it is a statement implying the existence of facts that support a legal opinion.
(2) A statement by an attorney is actionable as a fraudulent misrepresentation where it constitutes a direct factual assertion.
(3) A genuine issue of material fact is created by an attorney's statements that are actionable as fraudulent misrepresentations where there is a genuine issue of material fact as to whether the attorney either knew his statements were false when made or did not know whether they were true or false.

FACTS: Hoyt Properties (Hoyt) (P) brought an eviction action against Production Resource Group, L.L.C. (PRG) (D) and its subsidiary, Entolo. Hoyt (P) settled with Entolo and entered into release discussions with PRG (D), but before agreeing to release PRG (D) from liability, Hoyt's (P) owner had a conversation with PRG's (D) attorney. Hoyt's (P) owner said, "I don't know of any reason how we could pierce the [corporate] veil, do you?" Hoyt (P) alleged that PRG's (D) attorney responded, "There isn't anything. PRG and Entolo are totally separate." Hoyt (P) claimed that, relying on the statement made by PRG's (D) attorney, it agreed to release PRG (D). Subsequently, Hoyt (P) learned that a complaint in another action alleged contradictory facts that would support piercing the corporate veil. Hoyt (P) brought suit to rescind the release, claiming that PRG's (D) attorney's response had been a fraudulent misrepresentation. To succeed, Hoyt (P) would have to prove that the attorney's statement had been knowingly false and that Hoyt (P) had relied on it. The trial court dismissed the action on

summary judgment, but the state's intermediate appellate court reversed. The state's highest court granted review.

ISSUE:
(1) Is a statement made by an attorney actionable as a fraudulent misrepresentation where it is a statement implying the existence of facts that support a legal opinion?
(2) Is a statement by an attorney actionable as a fraudulent misrepresentation where it constitutes a direct factual assertion?
(3) Is a genuine issue of material fact created by an attorney's statements that are actionable as fraudulent misrepresentations where there is a genuine issue of material fact as to whether the attorney either knew his statements were false when made or did not know whether they were true or false?

HOLDING AND DECISION: (Page, J.)
(1) Yes. A statement made by an attorney is actionable as a fraudulent misrepresentation where it is a statement implying the existence of facts that support a legal opinion. PRG (D) argues that both parts of the attorney's response were legal opinions made in response to a question relating to a legal claim. PRG (D) contends that the use of the word "separate" in the attorney's second sentence is a legal term of art that "does not describe a particular factual predicate in a piercing-the-veil case, but rather, a general legal conclusion that piercing is not warranted." In contrast, Hoyt (P) asserted that the representation that "There isn't anything" implied that the attorney believed there was nothing about PRG's (D) and Entolo's business operations to justify a piercing claim. Hoyt (P) also asserted that the representation that "PRG (D) and Entolo are totally separate" was a direct factual statement bolstering the prior assertion that there were no facts supporting a veil-piercing claim. Under the summary judgment standard, the representations at issue must be viewed in the light most favorable to Hoyt (P). In such a light, the attorney's first sentence was a representation that no facts existed that would support a piercing claim. Even if that sentence was a legal opinion, it nevertheless implied that the attorney was aware of no facts supporting such a claim. Since the statement was not an expression of a pure legal opinion, but a statement implying the existence of facts supporting a legal opinion, the attorney's representation in the first sentence was actionable. Affirmed as to this issue.

Continued on next page.

(2) Yes. A statement by an attorney is actionable as a fraudulent misrepresentation where it constitutes a direct factual assertion. The representation made by the attorney's second sentence, when viewed in the light most favorable to Hoyt (P) under the summary judgment standard, is a direct factual assertion that the relationship between PRG (D) and Entolo was such that there were no facts to support a piercing claim. Accordingly, this representation is actionable. Affirmed as to this issue.

(3) Yes. A genuine issue of material fact is created by an attorney's statements that are actionable as fraudulent misrepresentations where there is a genuine issue of material fact as to whether the attorney either knew his statements were false when made or did not know whether they were true or false. For the attorney's statements to be fraudulent they must have been made with the attorney's knowledge of their falsity when made or made without knowing whether they were true or false. Here, whether the attorney knew his representations were false when made requires an assessment of the parties' credibility and weighing the evidence. These tasks cannot be done on summary judgment. Absent evidence in the record establishing, as a matter of law, that the representations were not knowingly false when made, there is a genuine issue of material fact for trial on that issue. There is also a genuine issue of material fact as to whether the attorney made the representations without knowing whether they were true or false. He knew about the complaint brought in the separate, third party action, which alleged facts that would support a piercing claim; however, he had not formed an opinion, one way or the other, about those alleged facts. This could lead a trier of fact to conclude that when the attorney made the representations, he did not know whether they were true. Affirmed as to this issue.

▶ ANALYSIS

Justice Anderson dissented, finding that because the first element of a claim for fraudulent misrepresentation is only met if the false factual representation by the party involves a "fact susceptible of knowledge," PRG's (D) attorney's representations could not be actionable. Justice Anderson reasoned that in order for the attorney to imply facts that "[t]here isn't anything" to a veil-piercing claim, the attorney would have to imply a factual assertion that the second prong of the piercing claim is met, i.e., that the claim is "necessary to avoid injustice or fundamental unfairness." Because this is a subjective inquiry made by a court, it is not a "fact susceptible of knowledge," and even if it were, it would be unreasonable to conclude that the attorney falsely implied that a veil-piercing claim would not meet this prong. In other words, if PRG's (D) attorney were to evaluate the claim and decide that it was viable, the attorney would have to conclude that it would be unjust and fundamentally unfair for the attorney's client to escape

liability. Those are not the type of conclusions an attorney is expected to make, and they are generally not susceptible of the attorney's knowledge. Similarly, because the two-prong test for piercing the corporate veil is a subjective test applied by the court, the attorney could not be in a position to know (1) what facts any particular court or factfinder might find significant, and (2) which factors under the first prong the court might apply, since the enumerated factors in case law are not exhaustive. Therefore, Justice Anderson found it difficult to see how the attorney could as a matter of law represent that "no facts" existed to support a piercing claim, given that a court could find a fact significant that no other court ever had in the past.

■—■—■

Quicknotes

CORPORATE VEIL Refers to the shielding from personal liability of a corporation's officers, directors or shareholders for unlawful conduct engaged in by the corporation.

ISSUE OF MATERIAL FACT A fact that is disputed between two or more parties to litigation that is essential to proving an element of the cause of action or a defense asserted, or which would otherwise affect the outcome of the proceeding.

SETTLEMENT AGREEMENT An agreement entered into by the parties to a civil lawsuit agreeing upon the determination of rights and issues between them, thus disposing of the need for judicial determination.

SUMMARY JUDGMENT Judgment rendered by a court in response to a motion made by one of the parties, claiming that the lack of a question of material fact in respect to an issue warrants disposition of the issue without consideration by the jury.

■—■—■

Virzi v. Grand Trunk Warehouse & Cold Storage Co.

Injured party (P) v. Company (D)

571 F. Supp. 507 (E.D. Mich. 1983).

NATURE OF CASE: Motion to set aside settlement in personal injury action.

FACT SUMMARY: Counsel for Virzi (P) obtained a settlement in his behalf, soon thereafter learned of his death, and failed to reveal same to opposing counsel and the court at a confirmation hearing.

RULE OF LAW
Counsel for a deceased party must inform opposing counsel and the court of his client's demise if such death is relevant to the litigation.

FACTS: Virzi (P) sued Grand Trunk Warehouse & Cold Storage Co. (Grand Trunk) (D) for personal injuries. Mediation was held. Unbeknownst to all involved, Virzi (P) had died of causes unrelated to the case several days prior to the mediation. The mediator valued the case at $35,000. Grand Trunk (D), on counsel's advice, accepted the figure. A hearing to confirm the settlement was held. Prior to the hearing, Virzi's (P) counsel became aware of Virzi's (P) death. He did not reveal this fact at the hearing because he was not so asked. The district court confirmed the settlement. Grand Trunk's (D) counsel learned of Virzi's (P) death and moved to set aside the settlement.

ISSUE: Must counsel for a deceased party inform opposing counsel and the court of his client's demise if such death is relevant to the litigation?

HOLDING AND DECISION: (Gilmore, J.) Yes. Counsel for a deceased party must inform opposing counsel and the court of his client's demise if such death is relevant to the litigation. While an attorney is under a clear duty not to make false assertions of fact to the court and opposing counsel, an attorney's duty of candor is higher than that. This candor involves a requirement of disclosing information essential to the merits of a suit, whether asked about the relevant facts or not. In this instance, whether or not Virzi (P) was alive was certainly a matter that went to the very essence of the value of the case, and counsel's failure to reveal Virzi's (P) demise constituted a sharp practice that cannot be condoned. Motion granted.

ANALYSIS

It is universally accepted that an attorney is under a duty to reveal adverse legal authority to a court. The obligation to reveal adverse facts is less clear. Lying to courts is, of course, prohibited, but the jurisdictions vary about the extent to which adverse information must be volunteered.

Quicknotes

ATTORNEY-CLIENT PRIVILEGE A doctrine precluding the admission into evidence of confidential communications between an attorney and his client made in the course of obtaining professional assistance.

CHAPTER 10

Lawyers for Companies and Other Organizations

Quick Reference Rules of Law

In re Grand Jury Subpoena

N/A

415 F.3d 333 (4th Cir. 2005).

NATURE OF CASE: Appeal from denial of motion to quash grand jury subpoenas.

FACT SUMMARY: Former employees of AOL (America Online) contended that grand jury subpoenas for documents related to an internal investigation conducted by AOL's attorneys should be quashed because the requested documents were protected by the attorney-client privilege and the joint defense privilege.

🏛 RULE OF LAW
(1) Conversations between a corporate employee and a corporation's attorneys during an internal investigation are not protected by the attorney-client privilege where the employee cannot show that an attorney-client relationship was formed during the investigation.
(2) Conversations between a corporate employee and a corporation's attorneys during an internal investigation are not protected by the joint defense privilege where the employee has entered into a common interest agreement with the company following the investigation.

FACTS: From March through June 2001, AOL (America Online) conducted an internal investigation into its relationship with PurchasePro, Inc. Outside counsel as well as in-house counsel conducted the investigation and interviewed AOL employees, including Wakeford, John Doe 1, and John Doe 2. The attorneys informed these employees that they represented AOL; that although the conversations were privileged, AOL could waive the privilege; and, if there was a conflict, the attorney-client privilege belonged to AOL. The attorneys also told the employees that either they could represent them, barring a conflict, or the employees could retain their own counsel, at AOL expense. In November, the Securities Exchange Commission (SEC) began to investigate AOL's relationship with PurchasePro. In December 2001, Wakeford and AOL, through counsel, entered into a "common interest agreement," which in part indicated that the disclosure of "Common Interest Materials" would not diminish the confidentiality of those materials or waive any applicable privilege. The employees testified before the SEC in 2002, and at their hearings, when questioned about their discussions with AOL attorneys during the March-June 2001 internal investigation, claimed that those discussions were protected by the attorney-client privilege. The employees indicated that they believed they were represented by the attorneys during those interviews. Two years later, a federal grand jury issued a subpoena commanding AOL to provide written memoranda and other written records reflecting the interviews of the employees conducted by the AOL attorneys from March to June 2001. AOL agreed to waive the attorney-client privilege and produce the subpoenaed documents, but the employees moved to quash the subpoena on the grounds that they each had an individual attorney-client relationship with the investigating attorneys, that their interviews were individually privileged, and that they had not waived the privilege. Wakeford also claimed that the information he disclosed to the investigating attorneys was privileged under the common interest doctrine. The district court denied the motions to quash, finding that in the case of all three employees none were clients of the investigating attorneys at the time of the interviews, and also denied Wakeford's motion on the ground that his common interest agreement with AOL postdated the interviews. The court based its conclusion on its findings that: (1) the investigating attorneys told the the employees that they represented the company; (2) the investigating attorneys told the the employees, "we represent you," not "we do represent you;" (3) the employees could not show that the investigating attorneys agreed to represent them; and (4) the investigating attorneys told the the employees that the attorney-client privilege belonged to AOL and AOL could choose to waive it. The court of appeals granted review.

ISSUE:
(1) Are conversations between a corporate employee and a corporation's attorneys during an internal investigation protected by the attorney-client privilege where the employee cannot show that an attorney-client relationship was formed during the investigation?
(2) Are conversations between a corporate employee and a corporation's attorneys during an internal investigation protected by the joint defense privilege where the employee has entered into a common interest agreement with the company following the investigation?

HOLDING AND DECISION: (Wilson, J.)
(1) No. Conversations between a corporate employee and a corporation's attorneys during an internal investigation are not protected by the attorney-client privilege where the employee cannot show that an attorney-client relationship was formed during the investigation. The essential elements for the formation of an attorney-client relationship between the investigating attorneys and the employees were missing at the time of the interviews. Despite the employees' subjective belief the attorneys were representing them personally, there was no evidence

Continued on next page.

of an objectively reasonable, mutual understanding that
the employees were seeking legal advice from the attorneys or that the attorneys were rendering personal legal
advice. This conclusion is supported by the attorneys'
disclosure to the employees that they represented AOL,
and that the privilege and the right to waive it were AOL's
alone. Moreover, the attorneys' statement to the employees that they could represent them absent a conflict was
not a statement that they were representing them. In
general, an individual's subjective belief that he is represented is not alone sufficient to create an attorney-client
relationship. Instead, that subjective belief must be reasonable under the circumstances. Here, under the circumstances, the employees could not reasonably have
believed that the investigating attorneys were representing them, given the attorneys' explicit disclaimers about
AOL being their client, that the privilege belonged to
AOL alone, and that they could, in theory represent
the employees (which in itself suggests that they were
not representing the employees at the time of the interviews). In addition, the employees never asked the attorneys to represent them, nor did the attorneys offer to do
so. Therefore, the district court did not err in finding that
no attorney-client relationship was established at the
time of the investigation, and, accordingly, the employees
do not have a privilege that they can assert. Affirmed as to
this issue.

(2) No. Conversations between a corporate employee and a
corporation's attorneys during an internal investigation
are not protected by the joint defense privilege where
the employee has entered into a common interest agreement with the company following the investigation.
The joint defense privilege is an extension of the attorney-client privilege, and serves to protect communications between parties who share a common interest in
litigation. The purpose of the privilege is to allow persons with a common interest to communicate with
their respective attorneys and with each other to
more effectively prosecute or defend their claims. For
the privilege to apply, the proponent must establish that
the parties had "some common interest about a legal
matter." An employee's cooperation in an internal investigation alone is not sufficient to establish a common
interest; rather "some form of joint strategy is necessary." The common interest agreement between AOL
and Wakeford did not exist prior to December 2001,
and these parties were not pursuing a joint legal strategy
before that time. Also, during the time of the internal
investigation, AOL would not have known whether its
interests were aligned with, or adverse to, those of
Wakeford. Accordingly, the district court did not err
in concluding that Wakeford did not have a joint defense privilege during the investigation or any time before December 2001. Affirmed as to this issue.

▶ ANALYSIS

If the investigating attorneys had in fact entered into an
attorney-client relationship with the employees, they would
not have been free to waive the employees' privilege when
a conflict arose, since ethically they could not place one
client's interests above those of another. Rather, the attorneys would have had to withdraw from all representation
and to maintain all confidences. As the court itself
observes, investigating counsel would not have been able
to robustly investigate and report to management or the
board of directors of a publicly-traded corporation with the
necessary candor if it were constrained by ethical obligations to individual employees. It is exactly for this reason
that courts are reluctant to find that investigating attorneys
who interview corporate employees or other corporate
constituents form an attorney-client relationship with
those interviewed. If they did, the investigating attorney
would be faced with multiple conflicts and would be
immobilized from conducting an investigation into wrongdoing.

Quicknotes

ATTORNEY-CLIENT PRIVILEGE A doctrine precluding the
admission into evidence of confidential communications
between an attorney and his client made in the course of
obtaining professional assistance.

ATTORNEY-CLIENT RELATIONSHIP The confidential relationship established when a lawyer enters into employment with a client.

QUASH To vacate, annul, void.

SUBPOENA A command issued by court to compel a
witness to appear at trial.

Tekni-Plex, Inc. v. Meyner & Landis

Manufacturing and packaging corporation (P) v. Attorneys (D)

N.Y. Ct. App., 89 N.Y.2d 123, 674 N.E.2d 663 (1996).

NATURE OF CASE: Appeal over a corporate acquisition involving counsel's duties to the company and its sole shareowner.

FACT SUMMARY: Tang wanted to retain the same counsel his old corporation used after he had sold the corporation to another company. The new owners sought to disqualify this counsel.

🏛 RULE OF LAW
Counsel cannot represent a present client against a former client involving matters that are substantially related to the prior representation and where the interests of the present client are materially adverse to the interests of the former client.

FACTS: Tom Tang was the president, chief executive officer, sole director, and sole shareholder of Tekni-Plex, Inc. Meyner & Landis (M&L) (D) represented Tang and Tekni-Plex on various legal matters, including securing an environmental permit for the operation of a laminator machine. Tang agreed to sell Tekni-Plex to the TP Acquisition Company (Acquisition). Acquisition was a shell corporation whose sole purpose was for the purchase of Tekni-Plex. Once the two corporations were merged Tekni-Plex would cease to exist and Acquisition would change its name to Tekni-Plex, Inc. (new Tekni-Plex) (P). Tang represented that old Tekni-Plex was in full compliance with all applicable environmental laws and possessed all requisite environmental permits. Tang and old Tekni-Plex was responsible for indemnification for any losses incurred by Acquisition as a result of misrepresentation. Following the merger, new Tekni-Plex (P) claimed that a laminator machine emitted volatile organic compounds and was therefore not allowed to operate. New Tekni-Plex (P) brought a claim against Tang for indemnification and Tang retained M&L (D) as counsel. New Tekni-Plex (P) sought to enjoin M&L (D) from representing Tang.

ISSUE: Can a long-time counsel for the seller company and its sole shareholder continue to represent the shareholder in a dispute with the buyer?

HOLDING AND DECISION: (Kaye, C.J.) No. Counsel cannot represent a present client against a former client involving matters that are substantially related to the prior representation and where the interests of the present client are materially adverse to the interests of the former client. The court ruled that new Tekni-Plex (P) had the burden of satisfying a three-pronged test for the disqualification of M&L (D). First, the court found that new Tekni-Plex (P) is a former client of M&L (D) since following the

merger, the business of old Tekni-Plex remained unchanged and consequently control of the attorney-client privilege passed to the hands of the new Tekni-Plex (P) management. Second, the court found that there was a substantial relationship between the current and former representations since the current dispute concerned the merger agreement on which the law firm had represented old Tekni-Plex. Third, the court concluded that the interests of M&L's (D) present (Tang) client were materially adverse to the interests of its former client (Tekni-Plex) because the claim set the purchaser's interest against Tang's interest as the seller. Because of the inherent conflicts of interest, M&L (D) were disqualified from representing Tang.

▶ ANALYSIS

Although the court found that new Tekni-Plex (P) is a former client of M&L (D) since it is essentially the same as old Tekni-Plex, it prohibited M&L (D) from releasing certain communications to new Tekni-Plex (P). These communications included Tang's confidences to M&L (D) during the merger negotiations. Giving new Tekni-Plex (P) this information would cause a chilling effect between attorneys and their clients since clients would worry that their privileged communications with counsel might later become available to others.

Quicknotes

ATTORNEY-CLIENT PRIVILEGE A doctrine precluding the admission into evidence of confidential communications between an attorney and his client made in the course of obtaining professional assistance.

CONFLICT OF INTEREST Refers to ethical problems that arise, or may be anticipated to arise, between an attorney and his client if the interests of the attorney, another client or a third party conflict with those of the present client.

DISQUALIFICATION A determination of unfitness or ineligibility.

Murphy & Demory, Ltd., et al. v. Admiral Daniel J. Murphy, U.S.N. (Ret.), et al.

Corporation (P) v. Former co-owner of corporation (D)

C.C. Va., Chancery No. 128219 (1994).

NATURE OF CASE: Legal malpractice action.

FACT SUMMARY: After Pillsbury (D), the law firm representing Murphy & Demory, Ltd. (P), assisted co-owner Murphy (D) in his efforts to take control of Murphy & Demory (P), Murphy & Demory (P) sued Pillsbury (D) for legal malpractice.

RULE OF LAW
Where dual representation of both a corporation and its individual owners presents a conflict of interest, the attorneys must obtain the corporation's consent for such representation after full disclosure of all material facts.

FACTS: Admiral Murphy (D) and Demory (P) co-owned Murphy & Demory, Ltd. (P). The law firm for Murphy & Demory Ltd. (P), Pillsbury, Madison & Sutro (Pillsbury) (D), through its attorneys Siemer (D) and Mendelson (D) assisted Murphy (D) in his efforts to take control of Murphy & Demory (P) or to form, before resigning from the company, a new corporation to compete with Murphy & Demory (P). Pillsbury (D) ignored its junior associates' warnings that the dual representation was rife with conflicts of interest, with possible breaches of fiduciary duty, and use of corporate opportunities. Murphy & Demory (P) filed suit against Admiral Murphy (D) and against Pillsbury (D).

ISSUE: Where dual representation of both a corporation and its individual owners presents a conflict of interest, must the attorneys obtain the corporation's consent for such representation after full disclosure of all material facts?

HOLDING AND DECISION: (Roush, J.) Yes. Where dual representation of both a corporation and its individual owners presents a conflict of interest, the attorneys must obtain the corporation's consent for such representation after full disclosure of all material facts. Here, Pillsbury (D) failed to disclose the conflict, to obtain consent for the dual representation of both Murphy (D) and Murphy & Demory, Ltd. (P), or, failing that, to withdraw from the representation. In concluding that there was no conflict, Siemer (D) willfully ignored the Rules of Professional Conduct. As a direct and proximate result of Pillsbury's (D) legal malpractice, Murphy & Demory, Ltd. (P) suffered compensatory damages in the amount of $500,000, and judgment is entered for that amount.

ANALYSIS

The court was particularly disturbed by the fact that every inquiry by an associate into the propriety of the firm's actions was referred to Siemer (D) for resolution. Siemer (D), the partner in charge of the client relationship affected by the issue, was the least likely to be objective, yet she was the ultimate arbiter of whether the firm had a conflict of interest. Mendelson (D) was held equally responsible for the legal malpractice since he was senior enough to have put a stop to the undisclosed dual representation.

Quicknotes

CONFLICT OF INTEREST Refers to ethical problems that arise, or may be anticipated to arise, between an attorney and his client if the interests of the attorney, another client or a third party conflict with those of the present client.

FIDUCIARY DUTY A legal obligation to act for the benefit of another, including subordinating one's personal interests to that of the other person.

CHAPTER 11

Judges

Quick Reference Rules of Law

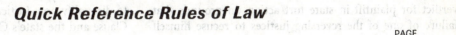

                                                PAGE

1. *Caperton v. A.T. Massey Coal Co.* Due process requires recusal of an elected judge where   *60*
the judge is deciding a case involving the interests of a contributor who by far made the
largest financial contribution to the judge's election campaign and otherwise played a pivotal
role in getting the judge elected, thus creating a "probability of bias."

2. *Liljeberg v. Health Services Acquisition Corp.* A judge, upon discovering a personal interest in   *63*
litigation, must recuse himself any time before final entry of judgment.

Caperton v. A.T. Massey Coal Co.

Business owner (P) v. Coal company (D)

556 U.S. 868 (2009).

NATURE OF CASE: Appeal from reversal of jury verdict for plaintiff in state tort action on grounds that failure of one of the reversing justices to recuse himself was an unconstitutional denial of due process.

FACT SUMMARY: A jury rendered a $50 million verdict against A.T. Massey Coal Co. and its affiliates (collectively, Massey) (D). Thereafter, the state was to hold its judicial elections. Massey's (D) chairman, Blankenship, became the largest contributor to Brent Benjamin's campaign for election to the state's highest court, and Benjamin was elected by a slim margin. Before the state's highest court was to hear the appeal in the case, Caperton and his affiliates (collectively, Caperton) (P) asked Benjamin to recuse himself based on the conflict caused by Blankenship's campaign involvement, but Benjamin refused, and continued to do so repeatedly. The state's highest court reversed the verdict. Caperton (P) asserted that Benjamin's failure to recuse himself was a due process violation.

RULE OF LAW

Due process requires recusal of an elected judge where the judge is deciding a case involving the interests of a contributor who by far made the largest financial contribution to the judge's election campaign and otherwise played a pivotal role in getting the judge elected, thus creating a "probability of bias."

FACTS: After a West Virginia jury found A.T. Massey Coal Co., a coal company, and its affiliates (collectively, Massey) (D), liable for fraudulent misrepresentation, concealment, and tortious interference with existing contractual relations and awarded Caperton, a business owner, and his affiliates (collectively, Caperton) (P) $50 million in damages, West Virginia held its 2004 judicial elections. The trial court denied Massey's (D) post-trial motions challenging the verdict and the damages award, finding that Massey (D) had intentionally acted in utter disregard of Caperton's (P) rights and ultimately destroyed Caperton's (P) businesses because, after conducting cost-benefit analyses, Massey (D) concluded it was in its financial interest to do so. Knowing the state's highest court, the West Virginia Supreme Court of Appeals, would consider the appeal, Blankenship, Massey's (D) chairman and principal officer, supported Brent Benjamin rather than the incumbent justice seeking reelection. Blankenship's $3 million in contributions exceeded the total amount spent by all other Benjamin supporters and by Benjamin's own committee. Benjamin won by fewer than 50,000 votes.

Before Massey (D) filed its appeal, Caperton (P) moved to disqualify now-Justice Benjamin under the Due Process Clause and the state's Code of Judicial Conduct, based on the conflict caused by Blankenship's campaign involvement. Justice Benjamin denied the motion, indicating that he found nothing showing bias for or against any litigant. The state's Supreme Court then reversed the $50 million verdict. During the rehearing process, Justice Benjamin refused twice more to recuse himself, and the court once again reversed the jury verdict. Four months later, Justice Benjamin filed a concurring opinion, defending the court's opinion and his recusal decision. The United States Supreme Court granted certiorari.

ISSUE: Does due process require recusal of an elected judge where the judge is deciding a case involving the interests of a contributor who by far made the largest financial contribution to the judge's election campaign and otherwise played a pivotal role in getting the judge elected thus creating a "probability of bias?"

HOLDING AND DECISION: (Kennedy, J.) Yes. Due process requires recusal of an elected judge where the judge is deciding a case involving the interests of a contributor who by far made the largest financial contribution to the judge's election campaign and otherwise played a pivotal role in getting the judge elected, thus creating a "probability of bias." The Due Process Clause incorporated the common-law rule requiring recusal when a judge has "a direct, personal, substantial, pecuniary interest" in a case. In addition, there are other instances, as an objective matter, which require recusal where "the probability of actual bias on the part of the judge or decision maker is too high to be constitutionally tolerable." One instance involved local tribunals in which a judge had a financial interest in a case's outcome that was less than what would have been considered personal or direct at common law. Another involved a state supreme court justice who cast the deciding vote upholding a punitive damages award while he was the lead plaintiff in a nearly identical suit pending in the state's lower courts. The proper constitutional inquiry was not "whether in fact [the justice] was influenced," but "whether sitting on [that] case . . . 'would offer a possible temptation to the average . . . judge to . . . lead him not to hold the balance nice, clear and true.'" Still another instance emerged in the criminal contempt context, where a judge had no pecuniary interest in the case but had determined in an earlier proceeding whether criminal charges should be brought and then proceeded to try and convict

Continued on next page.

the petitioners. In this regard, the Court has said "no man can be a judge in his own case," and "no man is permitted to try cases where he has an interest in the outcome." The judge's prior relationship with the defendant, as well as the information acquired from the prior proceeding, was critical. In reiterating that the rule that "a defendant in criminal contempt proceedings should be [tried] before a judge other than the one reviled by the contemnor," the Court noted that the objective inquiry is not whether the judge is actually biased, but whether the average judge in his position is likely to be neutral or there is an unconstitutional "potential for bias." Because the objective standards implementing the Due Process Clause do not require proof of actual bias Justice Benjamin's subjective findings of impartiality and propriety are not questioned, and there is no need to determine whether there was actual bias. Rather, the question is whether, "under a realistic appraisal of psychological tendencies and human weakness," the interest "poses such a risk of actual bias or prejudgment that the practice must be forbidden if the guarantee of due process is to be adequately implemented." Applying these principles here, there is a serious risk of actual bias when a person with a personal stake in a particular case had a significant and disproportionate influence in placing the judge on the case by raising funds or directing the judge's election campaign when the case was pending or imminent. The proper inquiry centers on the contribution's relative size in comparison to the total amount contributed to the campaign, the total amount spent in the election, and the apparent effect of the contribution on the outcome. It is not whether the contributions were a necessary and sufficient cause of Benjamin's victory. In an election decided by fewer than 50,000 votes, Blankenship's campaign contributions—compared to the total amount contributed to the campaign, as well as the total amount spent in the election—had a significant and disproportionate influence on the outcome. The risk that Blankenship's influence engendered actual bias is sufficiently substantial that it "must be forbidden if the guarantee of due process is to be adequately implemented." The temporal relationship between the campaign contributions, the justice's election, and the pendency of the case is also critical, for it was reasonably foreseeable that the pending case would be before the newly elected justice. The fear of bias arises in such a situation when—without the other parties' consent—a man seems to choose the judge in his own cause. Applying this principle to the judicial election process, there was here a serious, objective risk of actual bias that required Justice Benjamin's recusal. In other words, on these extreme facts, the probability of actual bias rises to an unconstitutional level. Massey (D) is mistaken in predicting that this decision will lead to adverse consequences ranging from a flood of recusal motions to unnecessary interference with judicial elections. The case at bar presents an extraordinary situation whose circumstances are extreme by any measure, and, because the States may have codes of conduct with more rigorous recusal standards than due process requires, most recusal disputes will be resolved without resort to the Constitution, making the constitutional standard's application rare. [Reversed and remanded.]

DISSENT: (Roberts, C.J.) The majority's decision will undermine—not promote—impartiality on the bench. The majority's "probability of bias" standard is too undefined to provide adequate guidance as to when recusal is constitutionally mandated, which will inevitably lead to an increase in allegations that judges are biased, however groundless those charges may be. Despite the majority's repeated emphasis on the need for an "objective" standard, the standard announced by the majority is too vague to be objective. Even if the majority is correct that the case at bar is extreme, it does not follow that claims of judicial bias will not be brought to test the "probability of bias" standard, since claims that have little chance of success are nonetheless frequently filed. Regardless of their merits, such claims will inevitably bring the accused judge, and the judicial system as a whole, into disrepute. Moreover, it is not at all clear that the case at bar is, in fact, an extreme case. Blankenship's contributions were overwhelmingly independent contributions over which Benjamin had no control, and there were many other indications that Benjamin's election had nothing to do with Blankenship's contributions, but rather was influenced by his opponent's gaffes, newspaper endorsements, and other factors (other than contributions) that normally affect elections.

DISSENT: (Scalia, J.) Instead of promoting the public's confidence in the judicial system, the majority's decision will have the opposite effect, since what above all else is eroding public confidence in the judicial system is the perception that litigation is just a game to be won by the most resourceful lawyers. The majority's decision, through its indefiniteness, will reinforce that perception, by engendering vast uncertainty and enabling endless litigation of nonrecusal decisions.

▎ *ANALYSIS*

In *Caperton,* the Court seemingly rejected the well-established appearances-based recusal standard in favor of a probability-based standard that examines the likelihood of actual bias. The appearances-based standard is employed by the federal recusal statutes as well as state judicial codes of conduct, and the issue before the Court was whether appearance of bias alone can rise to the level of a due process violation. Some courts—and Justice Benjamin himself—have taken the position that due process does not require recusal based on the appearance of bias alone, and that due process is implicated only where actual bias is shown. Others have taken the position that mere appearance of bias can violate due process, and some take the position that "appearance of bias" and

Continued on next page.

"probability of bias" are synonymous. By adopting the "probability of bias" standard, the majority arguably was aiming to avoid constitutionalizing the appearances-of-bias standard and to create an objective test based on the likelihood that a reasonable judge would actually be biased under a particular set of circumstances.

■■■■

Quicknotes

BIAS Predisposition; preconception; refers to the tendency of a judge to favor or disfavor a particular party.

DUE PROCESS The constitutional mandate requiring the courts to protect and enforce individuals' rights and liberties consistent with prevailing principles of fairness and justice and prohibiting the federal and state governments from such activities that deprive its citizens of life, liberty, or property interest.

RECUSAL Procedure whereby a judge is disqualified from hearing a case either on his own behalf, or on the objection of a party, due to some bias or interest on the part of the judge in the subject matter of the suit.

■■■■

Liljeberg v. Health Services Acquisition Corp.

Businessman (P) v. Corporation (D)

486 U.S. 847 (1988).

NATURE OF CASE: Review of order vacating judgment upon judge's failure to recuse.

FACT SUMMARY: A judge discovered, after he had rendered a verdict but before judgment became final, that he had a personal interest in the litigation.

🏛 RULE OF LAW
A judge, upon discovering a personal interest in litigation, must recuse himself any time before final entry of judgment.

FACTS: A contractual dispute arose between Liljeberg (P) and Health Services Acquisition Corp. (D) over the right to construct a hospital. Loyola University stood to benefit if Liljeberg (P) won. The judge to whom the case was assigned was a trustee of Loyola, although he apparently was unaware of Loyola's interest in Liljeberg's (P) success. After a bench trial, the judge announced a verdict in favor of Liljeberg (P). Several days later, before final entry of judgment, Loyola's interest was brought to the judge's attention. He denied a motion to vacate, and he entered judgment. The court of appeals reversed, holding that the judge should have recused himself immediately upon discovery of his interest. Liljeberg (P) petitioned for certiorari.

ISSUE: Must a judge, upon discovering personal interest in litigation, recuse himself any time before final entry of judgment?

HOLDING AND DECISION: (Stevens, J.) Yes. A judge, upon discovering a personal interest in litigation, must recuse himself any time before final entry of judgment. 28 U.S.C. § 455 provides that a judge shall disqualify himself in any proceeding in which his impartiality might be questioned. The section goes on to list a personal financial interest as a reason for such disqualification. Ill will or scienter is not a requirement for recusal; the section is designed to avoid even the appearance of bias. While a judge obviously cannot recuse himself for something he does not know, if such knowledge is imparted to him any time during the course of the action, a pall is cast over the whole proceeding, as such important motions as requests for new trials might be made right up to the time of final entry. For a judge to rule on such items with knowledge of a personal interest would undermine public confidence in the judiciary, an eventuality § 455 was drafted to prevent. Affirmed.

DISSENT: (Rehnquist, C.J.) The Court has used § 455 as a vehicle to compel judges to disqualify themselves for facts they do not know. It also broadens the standard for vacating final judgments under Fed. R. Civ. P. 60(b). These results are at odds with the intended scope of § 455 and Rule 60(b), and invite considerable mischief when courts attempt to apply them.

▶ ANALYSIS

The Court's ruling appears to have been broader in scope than necessary. In dicta, the Court seemed to say that § 455 encompasses a "should have known" standard. In this particular instance, the judge did acquire actual knowledge. The dissents took the Court to task for its broad holding.

Quicknotes

DICTUM Statement by a judge in a legal opinion that is not necessary for the resolution of the action.

SCIENTER Knowledge of certain facts; often refers to "guilty knowledge," which implicates liability.

28 U.S.C. § 455 A judge must recuse himself in any proceeding in which his impartiality might be questioned.

Control of Quality: Reducing the Likelihood of Professional Failure

Quick Reference Rules of Law

In re Glass

Bar applicant (P)

Cal. Sup. Ct., 316 P.3d 1199 (2014).

NATURE OF CASE: Review of bar application.

FACT SUMMARY: Stephen Randall Glass (P), a journalist made infamous by his fabricated stories, sources, and backgrounds, applied to the New York bar but withdrew when his moral character application was to be denied. He later applied to the California bar.

RULE OF LAW

An applicant cannot be accepted into a state bar if he or she commits ongoing acts or crimes involving moral turpitude.

FACTS: Stephen Randall Glass (P) was a journalist with *The New Republic* magazine. During his tenure, he fabricated more than 40 articles with many of the articles focused on denigrating ethnic and racial minority groups. Glass (P) lied about sources, settings, and quotes. He fabricated background and supporting material so the fact checkers at *The New Republic* would not catch him in his lies. Over time, his editor, Charles Lane, became suspicious and confronted Glass (P) about one of his stories. After confirming it was false and facing those who continued to support Glass (P), Lane fired Glass (P) and the truth came out. Glass (P) had attended law school during this time and applied to the New York bar. He did not detail each of his falsehoods and did not accept complete responsibility. His moral character application was to be denied, so he withdrew it. Two years later, he applied to the California bar and was more detailed about his transgressions. [His bar application progressed to a hearing at the state bar court.]

ISSUE: Can an applicant be accepted into a state bar if he or she commits ongoing acts or crimes involving moral turpitude?

HOLDING AND DECISION: (Per curiam) No. An applicant cannot be accepted into a state bar if he or she commits ongoing acts or crimes involving moral turpitude. The protection of clients and the judicial system necessitates a lawyer's strong moral character. Glass (P) engaged in a campaign of unremitting journalistic dishonesty over a period of years. He violated journalism's Code of Ethics and even has been embodied in a museum as one of the worst journalistic deceivers. It is reprehensible this conduct occurred while he studied law and sought a license to practice law. He harmed the public and his profession when he fabricated material for his articles. He could so much more harm his clients and the legal profession if he falsified evidence. His many character witnesses attest to his rehabilitation but compassion for him is not the standard for this court. It is the court's duty to protect the public and maintain the integrity of the profession. [Application denied.]

ANALYSIS

The state bar character application requires a recitation of every lapse in judgment a prospective attorney may have experienced. Most states are lenient as to the occasional traffic violation or a one-time failure, but repeated unethical behavior and a refusal to take responsibility does not bode well for an applicant.

Quicknotes

MORAL TURPITUDE Intentional conduct demonstrating depravity or vileness and which is contrary to acceptable and traditional societal behavior.

Leis v. Flynt

Ohio judges (D) v. Magazine publisher (P)

439 U.S. 438 (1979).

NATURE OF CASE: Review of order enjoining criminal prosecution.

FACT SUMMARY: Out-of-state counsel for Flynt (P) contended that a state court's summary denial of their request to appear pro hac vice was unconstitutional.

RULE OF LAW
Absent a governing rule or statute, a summary denial of a request to appear pro hac vice is not unconstitutional.

FACTS: Flynt (P) was charged in an Ohio state court with various criminal acts in connection with distribution of his Hustler magazine. Flynt (P) retained Fahringer and Cambria as counsel, neither of whom were admitted to practice in Ohio. They requested admission pro hac vice. Ohio had no governing law or rule regarding pro hac vice admission. The trial court summarily denied the request, and the Ohio Supreme Court denied mandamus. Flynt (P) filed an action in federal district court, contending that the summary denial was unconstitutional and requesting that prosecution be enjoined. The district court enjoined the prosecution until such time as the trial court held a hearing based on clear legal standards. The Sixth Circuit Court of Appeals affirmed, and the United States Supreme Court granted certiorari.

ISSUE: Is a summary denial of a request to appear pro hac vice unconstitutional absent a governing rule or statute?

HOLDING AND DECISION: (Per curiam) No. Absent a governing rule or statute, a summary denial of a request to appear pro hac vice is not unconstitutional. The Constitution does not create property interests; rather, it guarantees due process protection to rights created elsewhere. In the context of this case, the right to practice pro hac vice cannot be created by the Constitution, such right must arise elsewhere. In Ohio, there is no law or rule governing pro hac vice admissions. Consequently, there is no source of a substantive right to practice that the Constitution might protect. This being so Flynt's (P) due process argument with respect to pro hac vice admission fails. Reversed.

DISSENT: (Stevens, J.) An attorney has a property interest in pursuing his calling. A state may not arbitrarily deny an out-of-state attorney the right to practice law in its courts. The denial of Flynt's (P) counsels' request bore no rational relationship to the goal of guaranteeing professional competence.

ANALYSIS

Pro hac vice admissions are becoming more and more commonplace. This is a reflection of several trends in the law. Increasing specialization has led to the demand for specialists to practice across state lines. Also, the trend toward "megafirms" which practice in many jurisdictions has tended to promote lawyer mobility.

Quicknotes

DUE PROCESS The constitutional mandate requiring the courts to protect and enforce individuals' rights and liberties consistent with prevailing principles of fairness and justice and prohibiting the federal and state governments from such activities that deprive its citizens of a life, liberty or property interest.

PRO HAC VICE Applicable to a specific occasion; the use or application of a condition for the limited duration of a single situation.

Birbrower, Montalbano, Condon & Frank, P.C. v. Superior Court

Law firm (D/Petitioner), unlicensed in California, v. Court (Respondent); Corporation (P/Real Party in Interest)

Cal. Sup. Ct., 17 Cal. 4th 119, 949 P.2d 1, *cert. denied*, 525 U.S. 920 (1998).

NATURE OF CASE: Appeal from judgment that law firm practiced law without a license and was therefore not entitled to collect under fee agreement.

FACT SUMMARY: Birbrower, Montalbano, Condon & Frank, P.C. (Birbrower) (D/Petitioner), a New York law firm unlicensed to practice law in California, performed legal services for ESQ Business Services, Inc. (ESQ) (P/Real Party in Interest), a California-based corporation, without a license. ESQ (P) refused to pay, alleging malpractice and claiming that the firm could not collect its fee because of its unauthorized practice of law. Birbrower (D) counterclaimed for its fee.

RULE OF LAW
Advising a client and negotiating a settlement agreement in California without a license constitutes the unauthorized practice of law and no fee may be collected to the extent that the fee was for those services.

FACTS: ESQ Business Services, Inc. (ESQ) (P/Real Party in Interest), a California corporation, retained Birbrower, Montalbano, Condon & Frank, P.C. (Birbrower) (D/Petitioner), a New York law firm. None of the firm's attorneys were licensed to practice law in California. The fee agreement was negotiated and executed in New York, but provided that California law would govern all matters related to the representation. During several trips to California, the Birbrower (D) attorneys met with ESQ (P) and its accountants, gave legal advice, and made recommendations. They also spoke on their client's behalf during settlement agreement negotiations. ESQ (P) alleged malpractice, and Birbrower (D), counterclaimed to recover its fee.

ISSUE: Does it constitute the unauthorized practice of law for a New York law firm, not licensed in California, to perform legal services in California for a California client under a fee agreement stating that California law will control?

HOLDING AND DECISION: (Chin, J.) Yes. The court noted that the legal definition of "practicing law" included the giving of legal advice and the preparation of legal documents. The court then turned to the question of the meaning of "in California," holding that an unlicensed lawyer must engage in quantitatively sufficient activities within California or create a continuing attorney-client relationship for it to be determined that the attorney "practiced law in California." Although physical presence within the state is a factor, the court did not include that as a requirement in its analysis. Ruling that Birbrower's (D) actions constituted the extensive practice of law in California, the court declined to permit the firm from collecting its fee to the extent that the fee was based on any of the work it performed while in California. Affirmed in part, reversed in part, and remanded.

DISSENT: (Kennard, J.) This judge would define "practicing law" in a narrower way than the majority: "the representation of another in a judicial proceeding or an activity requiring the application of that degree of legal knowledge and technique possessed only by a trained legal mind." Because Birbrower's (D) activities while in California related only to arbitration, and arbitration is not necessarily "practicing law" under the above definition, the firm may have been entitled to relief.

ANALYSIS

The court recognized the distinction between the out-of-state litigator who obtains permission from a California judge to appear before that court pro hac vice and the out-of-state nonlitigator who cannot obtain similar authority to draft a legal document or provide legal advice to a client. Because case law offered no remedy for the nonlitigator who does not appear in a courtroom, the California legislature subsequently passed a law that permits, in effect, arbitrators the authority to admit out-of-state lawyers pro hac vice for in-state arbitrations.

Quicknotes

PRO HAC VICE Applicable to a specific occasion; the use or application of a condition for the limited duration of a single situation.

Linder v. Insurance Claims Consultants, Inc.

Insurance claimants (P) v. Insurance claim adjuster company (D)

S.C. Sup. Ct., 348 S.C. 477, 560 S.E.2d 612 (2002).

NATURE OF CASE: Action to declare contract void.

FACT SUMMARY: The Linders (P) contracted with Insurance Claims Consultants, Inc. (ICC) (D) for insurance adjustment services after property loss in a fire. ICC negotiated with the Linders' (P) insurance company about disputed claim payments and advised the Linders (P) about their coverage.

🏛 RULE OF LAW
Public insurance adjusters are not per se engaged in the unauthorized practice of law but may not engage in enumerated activities that require legal skill and knowledge.

FACTS: The Linders (P) suffered property damage in a fire. Their insurer did not approve their claim for full coverage of Mr. Linder's (P) gun collection. The Linders (P) contracted with Insurance Claims Consultants, Inc. (ICC) (D) to adjust their claims and agreed to pay ICC 10 percent of the total amount adjusted or recovered. ICC (D) advised the Linders (P) about their insurance coverage and policy language related to the gun collection and other claims. ICC (D) also engaged in negotiations with the insurer about claims. ICC (D) did get an increase of $12,000 claim payment to the Linders (P). The insurer delayed payment and the Linders (P), on advice of ICC (D), eventually retained counsel and then settled with the insurer. The Linders (P) refused to pay the 10 percent to ICC (D), so ICC (D) filed suit. The Linders (P) filed the instant action to declare the contract void because ICC (D) allegedly engaged in the unauthorized practice of law.

ISSUE: Are public insurance adjusters per se engaged in the unauthorized practice of law?

HOLDING AND DECISION: (Waller, J.) No. Public insurance adjusters are not per se engaged in the unauthorized practice of law but may not engage in enumerated activities that require legal skill and knowledge. This Court has exclusive jurisdiction to define the practice of law in South Carolina. The purpose of regulating the legal profession is not to economically benefit lawyers but to protect the public from the consequences of actions or advice of people untrained in the law. The line between the authorized practice of law and the permissible business activities of non-lawyers may be unclear. South Carolina has not previously examined whether the business activities of insurance adjusters constitute the unauthorized practice of law. [The court examined other states' decisions.] While the business of public insurance adjusting does not per se constitute the practice of law, certain activities in which adjusters may engage do constitute the practice of law. An adjuster can assess value, discuss that value, and engage in negotiations about value with the client and the insurer. None of that requires legal skill or expertise. Permissible insurance adjuster practices include estimating damage and repair costs, preparing inventories on proof of loss, presenting claims to insurers, and negotiating property-damage valuations. Prohibited activities include advising clients on interpretations of the policy language, advising clients on whether to accept settlement offers from an insurer, becoming involved in coverage disputes, or advertising the provision of services requiring legal skill. Here, ICC (D) did advise the Linders (P) on their rights under their policy and became involved in the coverage dispute over Mr. Linder's (P) gun collection. ICC (D) thus did engage in the unauthorized practice of law. Much of ICC's (D) work did not entail the practice of law, so it is entitled to recover for the value of that work. ICC (D) may not be compensated for any unauthorized activities and that is the appropriate sanction for its unauthorized practice of law.

DISSENT: (Pleicones, J.) Licensed public adjusters should be permitted to interpret insurance contracts, negotiate coverage disputes, and advise clients on whether to accept settlement offers. Adjusters have particular expertise in these areas and clients hire them for their specialized knowledge. The Linders (P) hired ICC (D) for its knowledge that the gun collection should be covered and ICC (D) should not be prohibited from advising when it knows of a coverage issue. Public insurance adjusters, however, should refrain from advising the client once attorneys or the legal system becomes involved in the matter.

▶ ANALYSIS

The "practice of law" is a fluid concept, but each state's highest court has the authority to determine what constitutes the practice of law as a matter of law within the state's borders. Some states are more restrictive with business practitioners than others when the practice veers too closely to legal advice. Businesses with specialized knowledge and skills may feel more qualified to advise clients in their area of expertise, but the consequences of poor advice can be severe. State supreme courts seek to protect the public from those consequences when they regulate the advice and services non-attorneys can provide.

CHAPTER 13

Control of Quality: Remedies for Professional Failure

Quick Reference Rules of Law

Togstad v. Vesely, Otto, Miller & Keefe

Paralysis victim (P) v. Law firm (D)

Minn. Sup. Ct., 291 N.W.2d 686 (1980).

NATURE OF CASE: Appeal of award of damages for legal malpractice.

FACT SUMMARY: Ms. Togstad (P) successfully sued Miller (D) of Vesely, Otto, Miller & Keefe (D) for legal malpractice, even though she had not formally retained him.

⚖ RULE OF LAW
A retainer is not required for an attorney-client relationship that may give rise to a malpractice claim to exist.

FACTS: Ms. Togstad (P) was rendered paralyzed after a medical procedure. Fourteen months later, Ms. Togstad (P) consulted with Miller (D) of Vesely, Otto, Miller & Keefe (D) regarding a possible malpractice action. After an initial consultation, Miller (D) informed Ms. Togstad (P) that he did not think she had a case, but that he would talk to his partners. Miller (D) never called back. After Minnesota's two-year statute of limitations on medical malpractice had expired, the Togstads (P) brought a legal malpractice action against Miller (D) for giving them erroneous advice and not advising them of the two-year statute. A jury found Miller (D) to have committed malpractice and awarded over $600,000 in damages. Miller (D) and his firm (D) appealed.

ISSUE: Is a retainer required for an attorney-client relationship that may give rise to a malpractice claim to exist?

HOLDING AND DECISION: (Per curiam) No. A retainer is not required for an attorney-client relationship that may give rise to a malpractice claim to exist. The first element in a malpractice claim is the existence of an attorney-client relationship. The crux of this relationship is the provision of advice by the attorney that he either knows or should know will be followed by the person to whom he provides the advice. This does not require actual retention. Here, Ms. Togstad (P) sought and obtained legal advice from Miller (D). It was entirely reasonable for Miller (D) to have expected the Togstads (P) to have followed his advice, which is exactly what they did. As a result, for purposes of a malpractice action, an attorney-client relationship between the Togstads (P) and Miller (D) existed. Affirmed.

▶ ANALYSIS

It is unclear as to whether the attorney-client relationship is defined by contract or tort theory. Appellate courts around the nation have gone both ways on this issue, on a variety of grounds. The court here recognized this diversity of opinion but did not indicate its preference for the one theory over the other. The court believed the contract and tort analyses for this case to be so similar that they did not need to be distinguished.

▄▀▄

Quicknotes

RETAINER Compensation paid in advance for professional services.

▄▀▄

Tante v. Herring

Attorney (D) v. Client seeking social security benefits (P)

Ga. Sup. Ct., 264 Ga. 694, 453 S.E.2d 686 (1994).

NATURE OF CASE: Action seeking damages against former counsel for legal malpractice, breach of fiduciary duty, and breach of contract.

FACT SUMMARY: Mrs. Herring (P) contended that Tante (D), her prior attorney, was liable for inducing her to have an affair with him.

🏛 RULE OF LAW
It is an actionable breach of fiduciary duty for an attorney to use information—available to him because of the attorney-client relationship—to his advantage and to the client's disadvantage.

FACTS: Tante (D) represented Mrs. Herring (P) in a Social Security Administration proceeding. During the course of his representation Mrs. Herring (P), who was married, had an affair with Tante (D). After the affair was over, the Herrings (P) sued Tante (D) for legal malpractice and breach of fiduciary duty, alleging that he used his knowledge of her fragile emotional state to induce her to have an affair, which had caused her emotional distress. The court of appeals held that the Herrings (P) could proceed on the breach of fiduciary duty claim. Tante (D) appealed.

ISSUE: Is it an actionable breach of fiduciary duty for an attorney to use information—available to him because of the attorney-client relationship—to his advantage and to the client's disadvantage?

HOLDING AND DECISION: (Hunt, C.J.) Yes. It is an actionable breach of fiduciary duty for an attorney to use information—available to him because of the attorney-client relationship—to his advantage and to the client's disadvantage. Even if Tante (D) was not guilty of malpractice in that his representation of Mrs. Herring (P) was competent, he still stands in a fiduciary relationship to her. If he used his superior knowledge to her detriment, he may be liable to the Herrings (P) for damages resulting from breach of the fiduciary duty to refrain from misusing confidential information. Accordingly, the Herrings (P) may pursue their claim. Affirmed.

▌ ANALYSIS

The problem encountered in this case presents several competing values. On the one hand, attorneys and their clients are consenting adults, who presumably have the capacity to make judgments about their relationships. On the other hand, the two are often unequal in terms of power, and the opportunity for exploitation is manifest. The states vary greatly as to how much leeway attorneys are given to engage in relationships with clients. Some prohibit it entirely. Others, like California, do not provide a blanket prohibition, but do not allow it in family law contexts, where a client may be particularly vulnerable emotionally.

Quicknotes

ATTORNEY-CLIENT PRIVILEGE A doctrine precluding the admission into evidence of confidential communications between an attorney and his client made in the course of obtaining professional assistance.

FIDUCIARY DUTY A legal obligation to act for the benefit of another, including subordinating one's personal interests to that of the other person.

Smith v. Haynsworth, Marion, McKay & Geurard

Real estate developer (P) v. Law firm (D)

S.C. Sup. Ct., 322 S.C. 433, 472 S.E.2d 612 (1996).

NATURE OF CASE: Appeal from defense verdict in malpractice action.

FACT SUMMARY: In a malpractice action against the legal firm Haynsworth, Marion, McKay & Geurard (D), the court excluded from evidence proffered testimony regarding violations of State Rules of Professional Conduct by the attorneys (D).

🏛 RULE OF LAW
Rules of Professional Conduct may be relevant in establishing legal malpractice.

FACTS: Smith (P) sued the firm Haynsworth, Marion, McKay & Geurard (D) over the latter's representation of him in a land development scheme that went sour. At trial, Smith (P) sought to introduce evidence that the firm (D) had violated state Rules of Professional Conduct. The court excluded this evidence. The jury returned a verdict in favor of Haynsworth, Marion, McKay & Geurard (D), and Smith (P) appealed.

ISSUE: May Rules of Professional Conduct be relevant in establishing legal malpractice?

HOLDING AND DECISION: (Waller, J.) Yes. Rules of Professional Conduct may be relevant in establishing legal malpractice. A plaintiff in a malpractice action must establish the standard of care that he alleges the attorney-defendant violated, and this must be done through expert testimony. Such an expert, generally an attorney or law professor, may rely on Rules of Professional Conduct as a standard by which to gauge the defendant's standard of conduct, so long as the rule whose violation is alleged was intended to protect a person in the position of the plaintiff. Here, the proffered testimony would appear to fall within this standard, so it should have been allowed. Reversed and remanded.

▌ANALYSIS

States vary widely as to the extent to which they allow the use of rules of professional conduct to be used as a standard in malpractice actions. Some exclude them entirely, concluding that they are more prejudicial than probative. Others make their violation malpractice per se. The approach taken here could be described as a middle course between these two positions.

Quicknotes

EXPERT TESTIMONY Testimonial evidence about a complex area of subject matter relevant to trial, presented by a person competent to inform the trier of fact due to specialized knowledge or training.

LOCALITY A defined geographic region; the circumscribed location that defines the reach of a court's authority.

Rodriguez v. Disner

[Parties not identified.]

688 F.3d 645 (9th Cir. 2012).

NATURE OF CASE: Appeal from denial of attorneys' fees in class action.

FACT SUMMARY: A law firm filed an antitrust class action and entered into "incentive agreements" with the named class members. The court determined this was a conflict of interest with the remaining class members and denied recovery of attorneys' fees.

🏛 RULE OF LAW
A court may consider an attorney's ethical misconduct, including its gravity, timing, willfulness, and effect on services, when awarding or denying attorney's fees.

FACTS: McGuire-Woods filed an antitrust class action against West Publishing. It then entered into "incentive agreements" with the named class members. The agreements provided payment to McGuire-Woods dependent upon the class recovery and recovery of $10 million provided the maximum payment of $75,000. The settlement provided a common fund of $49 million with 25 percent set aside for attorneys' fees. Certain class members from the remainder of the class objected to an award of any attorneys' fees because of McGuire-Woods' conflict of interest arising out of the incentive agreements. The district court first awarded fees of $7 million, but the Ninth Circuit Court of Appeals reversed and directed the court to consider the conflict of interest. On remand, the district court found McGuire-Woods had a conflict of interest constituting an ethical violation and it denied recovery of fees. McGuire-Woods appealed.

ISSUE: May a court consider an attorney's ethical misconduct when awarding or denying attorney's fees?

HOLDING AND DECISION: (Ikuta, J.) Yes. A court may consider an attorney's ethical misconduct, including its gravity, timing, willfulness, and effect on services, when awarding or denying attorney's fees. McGuire-Woods does not, nor could it, dispute it committed an ethical violation. As this court found in *Rodriguez I*, 563 F.3d. 948 (9th Cir. 2009), the incentive agreements tied counsel compensation to the amount recovered and thus created a disincentive for counsel to take the case to trial for a larger class recovery once the maximum fee of $75,000 had been achieved. This is a conflict position between the attorneys and the other members of the class. California Rule 3-310(C), the Rule 1.7(a) counterpart, prohibits representation when such a conflict exists. District courts have broad authority to consider ethical violations when determining an attorney award. If the violation is grave, an award may be denied. This is particularly important in common fund class action cases because the court has a special duty to protect the class interests. Denial of fees affirmed.

▶ ANALYSIS

The court's authority over the award of attorneys' fees rarely is limited even if the parties have an agreement contemplating a specific amount. An attorney's ethical misconduct would not be rewarded by the court with a fee award. McGuire-Woods perhaps could have received some award had it demonstrated it had obtained informed consent from the remainder of the class members when it created its conflict of interest.

Quicknotes

CONFLICT OF INTEREST Refers to ethical problems that arise, or may be anticipated to arise, between an attorney and his client if the interests of the attorney, another client or a third-party conflict with those of the present client.

Viner v. Sweet

Clients of attorney (P) v. Attorney (D)

Cal. Sup. Ct., 30 Cal. 4th 1232, 70 P.3d 1046 (2003).

NATURE OF CASE: Appeal from a damages award.

FACT SUMMARY: When the Viners (P) brought a malpractice action against their attorney, Sweet (D), for failure to properly prepare legal documents that would have protected the Viners (P), Sweet (D) argued that the plaintiff, in order to prevail in a transactional legal malpractice action, must prove that a more favorable result would have been obtained but for the alleged negligence.

RULE OF LAW
The plaintiff in a transactional legal malpractice action must prove that a more favorable result would have been obtained but for the alleged negligence.

FACTS: Michael and Deborah Viner (P) retained attorney Sweet (D) to draft various legal instruments in regard to their company, such as a securities purchase agreement and an employment termination agreement, which contained a noncompetition provision. In fact, the contracts failed to provide a variety of safeguards, which Sweet (D) had led the Viners (P) to believe were provided. Subsequently, disputes arose between the Viners (P) and companies with which they had contracted. Because the agreements failed to provide the protections that Sweet (D) had said were provided to the Viners (P), the Viners (P) alleged a large loss of income and consequently brought a malpractice action against Sweet (D). The jury awarded damages. The court of appeals reduced the damages award, but otherwise affirmed the judgment, stating that the "but for" test was inappropriate in a transactional legal malpractice action. Sweet (D) appealed, arguing that there is nothing distinctive about transactional malpractice to justify a relaxation of, or departure from, the well-established requirement in negligence cases that causation be established by the "but for" test.

ISSUE: Must the plaintiff in a transactional legal malpractice action prove that a more favorable result would have been obtained but for the alleged negligence?

HOLDING AND DECISION: (Kennard, J.) Yes. The plaintiff in a transactional legal malpractice action must prove that a more favorable result would have been obtained but for the alleged negligence. There is nothing distinctive about transactional malpractice to justify a relaxation of, or departure from, the well-established requirement in negligence cases that causation be established by the "but for" test. When a business transaction goes awry, a natural target of the disappointed principals is the attorneys who arranged or advised the deal. Clients predictably attempt to shift some part of the loss and disappointment of a deal that goes sour onto the shoulders of persons who were responsible for the underlying legal work. Before the loss can be shifted, however, the client has an initial hurdle to clear. It must be shown that the loss suffered was in fact caused by the alleged attorney malpractice. It is far too easy to make the legal advisor a scapegoat for a variety of business misjudgments unless the courts pay close attention to the cause in fact element, and deny recovery where the unfavorable outcome was likely to occur anyway, the client already knew the problems with the deal, or where the client's own misconduct or misjudgment caused the problems. It is the failure of the client to establish the causal link that explains decisions where the loss is termed remote or speculative. Courts are properly cautious about making attorneys guarantors of their clients' faulty business judgment. We do not agree with the court of appeals that litigation is inherently or necessarily less complex than transactional work. Some litigation, such as many lawsuits involving car accidents, is relatively uncomplicated, but so too is much transactional work, such as the negotiation of a simple lease or a purchase and sale agreement. But some litigation, such as a beneficiary's action against a trustee challenging the trustee's management of trust property over a period of decades, is as complex as most transactional work. Furthermore, an attorney's representation of a client often combines litigation and transactional work, as when the attorney effects a settlement of pending litigation. Reversed.

ANALYSIS

As the California Supreme Court points out in the *Viner* decision, the purpose of the "but for" requirement, which has been in use for more than 120 years, is to safeguard against speculative and conjectural claims. It serves the essential purpose of ensuring that damages awarded for the attorney's malpractice "actually have been caused by the malpractice."

Quicknotes

BUT FOR TEST For purposes of determining tort liability the test for the element of causation is whether the plaintiff would not have suffered the injury "but for" the defendant's conduct.

Continued on next page.

FIDUCIARY DUTY A legal obligation to act for the benefit of another, including subordinating one's personal interests to that of the other person.

PROFESSIONAL NEGLIGENCE The breach of a fiduciary duty owed to one's client, caused by the professional's actions and injurious to the client.

Peeler v. Hughes

Corporate officer (P) v. Law firm (D)

Tex. Sup. Ct., 909 S.W.2d ...

NATURE OF CASE: Appeal from dismissal of malpractice action.

FACT SUMMARY: Peeler (P), who had accepted a plea bargain in a prosecution in which Hughes & Luce (D) defended her, sued the firm for malpractice when she learned that a prosecutorial offer of immunity had not been communicated to her.

RULE OF LAW:
A legal malpractice claim may not be brought in the context of a criminal matter absent a showing that the plaintiff has been exonerated from the conviction.

FACTS: Peeler (P) and her husband were indicted on numerous counts of tax-related crimes. She eventually accepted a plea bargain in which all but one of the charges against her were dropped, resulting in a short sentence and a fine. Subsequent to pleading guilty, she discovered that the prosecutor had conveyed to her attorney at Hughes & Luce (D) an offer of absolute transactional immunity in exchange for testifying against alleged co-conspirators. This offer had never been communicated to her. She sued Hughes & Luce (D) for malpractice. The trial court granted Hughes & Luce (D) a motion for summary judgment, dismissing the action. The court of appeals affirmed, and the state supreme court granted review.

ISSUE: May a legal malpractice claim be brought in the context of a criminal matter absent a showing that the plaintiff has been exonerated from the conviction?

HOLDING AND DECISION: (Gonzalez, J.) No. A legal malpractice claim may not be brought in the context of a criminal matter absent a showing that the plaintiff has been exonerated from the conviction. This is because a criminal defendant, absent a showing that the plaintiff has been exonerated from the conviction, must have had his conduct be the sole cause of any injury suffered as a result of conviction. Therefore, the only time a plaintiff can regas the sole proximate cause, but to show a cause of action for professional negligence. Thus a criminal defendant who has been found guilty, either by plea or verdict, cannot sue his attorney for malpractice unless the conviction is later overturned on direct appeal or collateral attack. Held otherwise, it would allow the criminal to profit from his misdeed, something the law cannot countenance. In this instance, Peeler (P) was convicted through a guilty plea but never even asserted that she did not commit the acts for which she was indicted, so she has no action against Hughes & Luce (D). Affirmed.

CONCURRENCE: (Hightower, J.) In the instant case, it may be that as conducting the alleged ...

DISSENT: (Phillips, C.J.) An exception to the rule cited by the court should be made when it can be shown that but for the alleged malpractice, the defendant would not have been convicted.

ANALYSIS

The rule cited here leaves a hapless convict with some-thing of a Catch-22. If his attorney's malpractice lands him in prison, he has no recourse against the attorney. The only hope for one in a position such as Peeler (P) found himself would be appeal or habeas proceeding based on ineffective counsel in violation of the Sixth Amendment. However, even this remedy is probably unavailable to one who pleabargains.

Quicknotes

PROFESSIONAL NEGLIGENCE The breach of a fiduciary duty owed to one's client, caused by the professional's actions and injurious to the client.

PROXIMATE CAUSE The natural sequence of events without which an injury would not have been sustained.

TRANSACTIONAL IMMUNITY Also called the privilege against self-incrimination, a person's constitutional right to refuse to render testimony that may incriminate them if called as a witness.

Peeler v. Hughes & Luce

Corporate officer (P) v. Law firm (D)

Tex. Sup. Ct., 909 S.W.2d 494 (1995).

NATURE OF CASE: Appeal from dismissal of malpractice action.

FACT SUMMARY: Peeler (P), who had accepted a plea bargain in a prosecution in which Hughes & Luce (D) defended her, sued the firm for malpractice when she learned that a prosecutorial offer of immunity had not been communicated to her.

🏛 RULE OF LAW
A legal malpractice claim may not be brought in the context of a criminal matter absent a showing that the plaintiff has been exonerated from the conviction.

FACTS: Peeler (P) and her husband were indicted on numerous counts of tax-related crimes. She eventually accepted a plea bargain in which all but one of the charges against her were dropped, resulting in a short sentence and a fine. Subsequent to pleading guilty, she discovered that the prosecutor had conveyed to her attorney at Hughes & Luce (D) an offer of absolute transactional immunity in exchange for testifying against alleged co-conspirators. This offer had never been communicated to her. She sued Hughes & Luce (D) for malpractice. The trial court granted Hughes & Luce's (D) motion for summary judgment, dismissing the action. The court of appeals affirmed, and the state supreme court granted review.

ISSUE: May a legal malpractice claim be brought in the context of a criminal matter absent a showing that the plaintiff has been exonerated from the conviction?

HOLDING AND DECISION: (Enoch, J.) No. A legal malpractice claim may not be brought in the context of a criminal matter absent a showing that the plaintiff has been exonerated from the conviction. This is because criminal conduct is the only cause of any injury suffered as a result of conviction. Therefore only innocent plaintiffs can negate the sole-proximate-cause bar to their cause of action for professional negligence. Thus a criminal defendant who has been found guilty, either by plea or verdict, cannot sue his attorneys for malpractice unless the conviction is later overturned on direct appeal or collateral attack. To hold otherwise would allow the criminal to financially profit from his misdeed, something the law cannot countenance. In this instance, Peeler (P) was convicted through a guilty plea and never even asserted that she did not commit the acts for which she was indicted, so she has no action against Hughes & Luce (D). Affirmed.

CONCURRENCE: (Hightower, J.) The holding today should not be read as condoning the alleged malfeasance of Peeler's (P) attorney which, if true, was reprehensible and unconscionable.

DISSENT: (Phillips, C.J.) An exception to the rule cited by the court should be made when it can be shown that, but for the alleged malpractice, the defendant would not have been convicted.

▌ANALYSIS

The rule cited here leaves a hapless convict with something of a Catch-22: If his attorney's malpractice lands him in prison, he has no recourse against the attorney. The only hope for one in a position such as Peeler (P) found herself would be appeal or habeas proceeding based on ineffective counsel in violation of the Sixth Amendment. However, even this remedy is probably unavailable to one who plea bargains.

■=■

Quicknotes

PROFESSIONAL NEGLIGENCE The breach of a fiduciary duty owed to one's client, caused by the professional's actions and injurious to the client.

PROXIMATE CAUSE The natural sequence of events without which an injury would not have been sustained.

TRANSACTIONAL IMMUNITY Also called the privilege against self-incrimination; a person's constitutional right to refuse to render testimony that may incriminate them if called as a witness.

■=■

Mashaney v. Board of Indigents' Defense Services

Criminal malpractice claimant (P) v. [Not identified in excerpt]

Kan. Sup. Ct., 355 P.3d 667 (2015).

NATURE OF CASE: Appeal in legal malpractice action.

FACT SUMMARY: Mashaney (P) filed a legal malpractice action against his trial and appellate lawyers but could not prove actual innocence because he entered an *Alford* plea to lesser charges.

> **RULE OF LAW**
> Public policy does not require a criminal malpractice plaintiff to prove actual innocence in addition to winning exoneration.

FACTS: Mashaney (P) was convicted and sentenced to 442 months imprisonment. Seven years later, his conviction was vacated and he entered an *Alford* plea to lesser charges. His sentence was reduced to 72 months. Mashaney (P) filed a legal malpractice claim against his trial and appellate attorneys. [Mashaney (P) appealed to the intermediate appellate court.] Mashaney (P) was required to win exoneration and prove actual innocence to succeed in his claim. Mashaney (P) could not meet the actual innocence burden because he had entered the *Alford* plea. Mashaney (P) appealed to the state supreme court.

ISSUE: Does public policy require a criminal malpractice plaintiff to prove actual innocence in addition to winning exoneration?

HOLDING AND DECISION: [Judge not identified in casebook excerpt.] No. Public policy does not require a criminal malpractice plaintiff to prove actual innocence in addition to winning exoneration. [The state supreme court relied on and quoted the dissent filed by Judge G. Gordon Atcheson in the intermediate appellate decision]: Proponents of the actual innocence requirement rely on a rigid application of "but for" causation in which the incarceration is the result of the convicted criminal defendant's crime rather than the incompetency of the defense counsel. This application is inconsistent with general tort law principles, which look to proximate cause to impose liability. The proximate cause of the incarceration would be the failure of the defense lawyer to demonstrate the state's inability to prove the case beyond a reasonable doubt when a competent lawyer would have so demonstrated. The same harm would have been suffered by an innocent person, so the actual guilt of the defendant is not relevant. Proximate cause also requires foreseeability of the harm and a defense attorney certainly can foresee that incompetent representation could result in incarceration of the client. Tort law does not carve out exceptions for physicians or civil attorneys, so no such exception should

exist for criminal attorneys. Advocates for an actual innocence requirement also claim criminal defendants might profit from their own wrongs if they can sue their lawyers for malpractice although guilty of the crime. There is no profit here, however; the criminal defendant is being compensated for the legal injury of incarceration directly resulting from a lawyer's malpractice. Arguably, Henry Hill profited from his participation in a biography and film about his mob career, and that is a profit from wrongdoing. The stated concern that attorneys will not take on criminal defendants is without merit. States such as Indiana and Ohio treat civil and criminal malpractice claims equally and there is no shortage of lawyers handling criminal cases in those states. Kansas further requires a criminal defendant win exoneration prior to even filing a legal malpractice claim. This requirement should preclude criminal defendants filing malpractice claims without substantial supporting allegations. The actual innocence rule does not advance public policy or facilitate resolution of malpractice claims based on tort law. It instead reflects a policy of depriving criminal defendants of a civil remedy against their lawyers when abysmal performance resulted in incarceration. Criminal defendants have a right to competent representation and the judicial process should provide an opportunity for full recompense if a violation of that right results in conviction and incarceration. [Decision not included in casebook excerpt.]

◢ ANALYSIS

The Kansas Supreme Court rejected the actual innocence rule for Kansas. With respect to Mashaney (P), the Court permitted his legal malpractice claim to proceed although it agreed with Judge Atcheson that Mashaney (P) may not be able to meet his burden of proof on the legal malpractice elements for other reasons. Kansas now recognizes the same standard for civil and criminal malpractice claims once a convicted criminal defendant has won exoneration.

■■■

Quicknotes

"BUT FOR" TEST For purposes of determining tort liability, the test for the element of causation is whether the plaintiff would not have suffered the injury "but for" the defendant's conduct.

FORESEEABILITY OF HARM An inquiry into the relatedness of events that contributed to the plaintiff's injury; whether

Continued on next page.

the harm was foreseeable determines whether the tort-feasor's conduct was the proximate cause of the injury.

INEFFECTIVE ASSISTANCE OF COUNSEL A claim brought by an accused in which it must be determined whether the attorney's rendering of representation was such that the ultimate disposition of the case may not be relied upon as fair.

PROXIMATE CAUSE The natural sequence of events without which an injury would not have been sustained.

Petrillo v. Bachenberg

Land purchaser (P) v. Real estate broker (D)

N.J. Sup. Ct., 139 N.J. 472, 655 A.2d 1354 (1995).

NATURE OF CASE: Review of order reversing dismissal of negligent misrepresentation claim.

FACT SUMMARY: Petrillo (P) sued attorney Herrigel (D) for preparation of a misleading composite report even though Herrigel (D) had never represented her.

🏛 RULE OF LAW
Attorneys may owe a duty of care to nonclients when the attorneys know, or should know, that nonclients will rely on the attorneys' representations and the nonclients are not too remote from the attorneys to be entitled to protection.

FACTS: Developer Rohrer Construction and its attorney, Herrigel (D), solicited from a soils engineer tests regarding the suitability of certain real estate for the placement of a septic system. Two series of tests were performed that indicated that the land was unsuitable. A report was compiled from the two series of tests that gave the impression that the land was in fact suitable. The land was eventually purchased at a foreclosure sale by Bachenberg (D), who then retained Herrigel (D), who passed on to him the erroneous report. The land was then sold to Petrillo (P) for commercial development. Petrillo (P), who had been given a copy of the report during her negotiations to purchase the property, hired an engineering firm to conduct her own tests, which showed that the land could not be brought into compliance with local ordinances and was undevelopable. She then sued Bachenberg (D) for return of the purchase money, and Herrigel (D) for providing the erroneous report. The trial court dismissed the claim against Herrigel (D), but the court of appeals reversed. The New Jersey Supreme Court granted review.

ISSUE: May attorneys owe a duty of care to nonclients?

HOLDING AND DECISION: (Pollock, J.) Yes. Attorneys may owe a duty of care to nonclients when the attorneys know, or should know, that nonclients will rely on the attorneys' representations and the nonclients are not too remote from the attorneys to be entitled to protection. At common law, an attorney was not liable to a nonclient due to lack of privity. This rule has slowly been replaced with one that looks more to the overall circumstances to ascertain whether the attorney should have liability imposed on him for injury to a nonclient. Generally speaking, if a lawyer negligently prepares a document and such document is foreseeably to be used by third parties, such parties have recourse against the attorney. Examples of such situations include opinion letters and securities offering statements. Here, it was foreseeable that a purchaser of the property would rely on the soils report in making a purchase decision, so Herrigel's (D) duty extended to Petrillo (P). A jury should have the opportunity to decide the effect of Herrigel's (D) alleged negligent misrepresentation. Affirmed.

DISSENT: (Garibaldi, J.) As Petrillo (P) did not rely on any opinion offered by Herriger (D), he owed no duty of care to her.

▶ ANALYSIS

The Washington Supreme Court has formulated a balancing test to determine when lawyers may be held liable to nonclients. Factors to be considered include the extent to which the transaction was intended to benefit the plaintiff, the foreseeability of harm to the plaintiff, and the closeness of the connection between the defendant's conduct and the injury. Policy considerations include prevention of future harm and the extent to which the legal profession would be unduly burdened by a finding of liability. See *Trask v. Butler*, 872 P.2d 1080 (1994).

Quicknotes

DUTY OF CARE A principle of negligence requiring an individual to act in such a manner as to avoid injury to a person to whom he or she owes an obligatory duty.

PRIVITY Commonality of rights or interests between parties.

In re Warhaftig

N/A

N.J. Sup. Ct., 106 N.J. 529, 524 A.2d 398 (1987).

NATURE OF CASE: Attorney disciplinary proceeding.

FACT SUMMARY: Warhaftig (D) appropriated client funds, although he did so with the intention of repaying the funds.

🏛 RULE OF LAW
An attorney may be disbarred for taking fee advances out of client funds, even if he did so with the intention of returning the funds.

FACTS: Attorney Warhaftig (D), faced with serious financial pressures, began appropriating client funds. For the most part, the funds were returned. When the State Bar (P) discovered Warhaftig's (D) activities, it instituted disciplinary proceedings. Warhaftig (D) argued in his defense that he had only meant to "borrow" the monies taken, not permanently misappropriate them. Based on this distinction, the State Bar (P) recommended a reprimand but not disbarment. The state supreme court reviewed the conclusions.

ISSUE: May an attorney be disbarred for taking fee advances out of client funds, even if he did so with the intention of returning the funds?

HOLDING AND DECISION: (Per curiam) Yes. An attorney may be disbarred for taking fee advances out of client funds, even if he did so with the intention of returning the funds. This court has ruled that an attorney who knowingly misappropriates client funds must be disbarred. The distinction made by the State Bar (P) in this instance is misplaced. Misappropriation is prohibited, whether or not the funds are "stolen" or "borrowed." A bank teller can hardly use this excuse if his employer finds him taking funds, and an attorney should be held to at least as high a standard. Here, Warhaftig (D) knowingly took funds to which he was not entitled, and this ends the inquiry. [The court then held mitigating factors to be insufficient, and ordered Warhaftig (D) disbarred.]

▶ ANALYSIS

The court did admit that Warhaftig (D) may not have been as culpable as if he had had no intent to repay his client's money, but the court found the difference to be only negligible. Of course, to trigger automatic disbarment, the misappropriation must be "knowing." Merely careless bookkeeping or accidental use of client monies will not subject an attorney to disbarment, but may result in sanctions for failure to protect client property.

Quicknotes

DISBARMENT The administrative penalty levied against an attorney for a breach of professional conduct that effectively revokes the license to practice law.

MISAPPROPRIATION The unlawful use of another's property or funds.

In re Disciplinary Proceedings Against Siderits

[Party not identified] (P) v. Law firm partner (D)

Wis. Sup. Ct., 824 N.W.2d 812 (2013).

NATURE OF CASE: Disciplinary action.

FACT SUMMARY: Siderits (D) manipulated his billed time at his firm to receive unearned bonus compensation. He then "wrote down" the time so no clients ever paid for the fabricated time.

 RULE OF LAW
An attorney's ignorance of the law does not excuse an ethics violation.

FACTS: Attorney Siderits (D) was a partner at his law firm and only eligible for an annual bonus if he billed at least 1,800 hours. Siderits (D) would bill the time even though he did not really work, collect the bonus, and then "write down" the time so that no client was ever billed for the fabricated time. Siderits (D) collected nearly $47,000 in unearned bonuses.

ISSUE: Does an attorney's ignorance of the law excuse an ethics violation?

HOLDING AND DECISION: (Per curiam) No. An attorney's ignorance of the law does not excuse an ethics violation. Siderits (D) claimed he was denied due process because his firm had no written policy regarding writing down time and he could not know it was prohibited. He also argued he was unaware of this court's determination that a lawyer's misappropriation of funds from a law firm is the same as that taken from a client. His ignorance is no excuse. The prohibition against stealing from one's law firm does not require a written policy and should be readily ascertained. Siderits's (D) employment has been terminated, he has lost his equity interest in the firm, he has repaid the firm $60,000 for the bonuses and other claims, and he is responsible for nearly $19,000 in costs for the disciplinary proceedings. Siderits (D) is suspended from the practice of law for one year.

▶ ANALYSIS

Courts do not permit criminal defendants to assert ignorance as a valid defense, so neither should attorneys be permitted to claim ignorance of ethical obligations and cases. Allowing it could encourage willful ignorance where attorneys might deliberately avoid becoming familiar with professional rules of conduct.

Quicknotes

DUE PROCESS The constitutional mandate requiring the courts to protect and enforce individuals' rights and liberties consistent with prevailing principles of fairness and justice and prohibiting the federal and state governments from such activities that deprive its citizens of life, liberty, or property interest.

MISAPPROPRIATION The unlawful use of another's property or funds.

Stropnicky v. Nathanson

Male potential client (P) v. Attorney (D)

Massachusetts Commission Against Discrimination (Feb. 25, 1997).

NATURE OF CASE: Commission review of discrimination complaint.

FACT SUMMARY: Joseph Stropnicky (P) filed a complaint of discrimination against Attorney Nathanson (D) when she refused to represent him because of his gender. Attorney Nathanson (D) only represented women in divorce proceedings.

🏛 RULE OF LAW
A Massachusetts attorney may not refuse to represent a potential client based solely on that client's membership in a protected class.

FACTS: Attorney Nathanson (D) only represented women in divorce proceedings. Joseph Stropnicky (P) and his wife were divorcing and Stropnicky (P) contacted Nathanson's (D) office for representation. Nathanson (D) informed him of her women-only divorce practice. Stropnicky (P) informed Nathanson (D) his personal circumstances were more similar to those of women because he had been the stay-at-home caretaker with significantly less income-generation while his wife was a successful physician making ten times his teacher salary. Nathanson (D) made no exception and would not represent him because he is a male. Stropnicky (P) filed a charge with the Massachusetts Commission Against Discrimination.

ISSUE: May a Massachusetts attorney refuse to represent a potential client based solely on that client's membership in a protected class?

HOLDING AND DECISION: [Commn. not listed in casebook excerpt.] No. A Massachusetts attorney may not refuse to represent a potential client based solely on that client's membership in a protected class. Nathanson (D) argues her divorce practice is limited to women because of specific considerations affecting women in a traditionally gender-biased judicial system. Her limited practice offers her specialization in women's issues and respect with the family court judges. This holding is not meant to regulate an attorney's areas of practice. It is acceptable if an attorney declines representation because the issues are not in his or her specialty or for traditional business considerations. It is not acceptable for an attorney to refuse to represent a client solely based on his gender. This case would appear more starkly to be a violation had this been a female or an African-American but it still constitutes unlawful discrimination. [Nathanson (D) was ordered to pay Stropnicky (P) $5,000.]

▶ ANALYSIS

On appeal, the full Commission affirmed the decision. Critics argued women do have different needs and issues in the judicial system and focusing on gender-based representation is no different than choosing to focus on plaintiff-based representation. The Massachusetts law, however, does not permit discrimination based on gender and does permit discrimination based on other factors (e.g., plaintiff versus defendant, employee versus management, landlord versus tenant).

Quicknotes

GENDER DISCRIMINATION Unequal treatment of individuals without justification on the basis of their sex.

■=■

In re Jordan Schiff
N/A

Departmental Disciplinary Committee, N.Y. Sup. Ct., Docket No. HP 22/92 (1993).

NATURE OF CASE: Disciplinary action taken in response to allegations of misconduct by an attorney during a deposition.

FACT SUMMARY: This disciplinary hearing was held after Schiff (D) allegedly violated the code of ethics by using obscene, explicit, gender-specific vulgarities to harass opposing female counsel during a deposition.

🏛 **RULE OF LAW**
Attorneys who direct dirty, discriminatory, gutter language at opposing counsel to harass counsel on the basis of gender will be subject to sanction for violation of the rules of professional ethics.

FACTS: During a deposition of a client which his firm represented in a personal injury suit, Schiff (D) used obscene, explicit, gender-specific vulgarities in an attempt to intimidate and harass opposing counsel, Mark (P). Early in the deposition, a senior partner of Schiff's (D) firm had set the tone by standing and shouting at Mark (P). During a hearing held by the Disciplinary Committee, both the court reporter and the Spanish interpreter testified that, off the record, Schiff (D) referred to Mark (P) as a "cunt" and an "asshole" and said she should "go home and have babies." On the record, the deposition itself was replete with sexual obscenities uttered by Schiff (D).

ISSUE: Will attorneys who direct dirty, discriminatory, gutter language at opposing counsel to harass counsel on the basis of gender be subject to sanction for violation of the rules of professional ethics?

HOLDING AND DECISION: (Elsen, Panel Chair) Yes. Attorneys who direct dirty, discriminatory, gutter language at opposing counsel to harass counsel on the basis of gender will be subject to sanction for violation of the rules of professional ethics. In mitigation, Schiff (D) apologized to Mark (P) by letter and at the hearing. However, the record shows that the apology and sanctions imposed on Schiff's (D) law firm were insufficient to convince him that his conduct was in need of reform. Evidence of a later deposition in another case reveals Schiff (D) used gender-specific vulgarities again in speaking to opposing female counsel. On the evidence presented, all charges against Schiff (D) of ethics violations are sustained. The sanction will be public censure.

▶ **ANALYSIS**

The panel declared that were it not for Schiff's (D) unblemished record and his youth, plus the consideration that he was no longer with the firm that set him such a bad example, their recommendation would be even more severe. Public censure was deemed appropriate because those in the profession must understand that sexual harassment is unacceptable, and the public must understand that the profession abhors such behavior and will not condone it. In censuring Schiff (D), *In Re Schiff*, 190 A.D.2d 293 (1993), the court described his conduct as "inexcusable and intolerable, reflecting adversely on his fitness to practice law."

Quicknotes

PUBLIC CENSURE A statement issued by a governing body toward one of its members officially reprimanding that person, and carrying a higher degree of professional disgrace than a simple reprimand because it is made public.

Strickland v. Washington

Convicted murderer (D) v. State (P)

466 U.S. 668 (1984).

NATURE OF CASE: Review of death sentence imposed subsequent to murder conviction.

FACT SUMMARY: Strickland (D) challenged his death sentence on the ground the lawyer who represented him at the hearing was constitutionally ineffective.

RULE OF LAW
A court deciding on ineffectiveness of counsel claim at a death sentence hearing must judge whether counsel's conduct was reasonable under the facts as viewed at the time of the alleged ineffectiveness.

FACTS: Strickland (D) was charged and convicted of murder. Per Washington law, a hearing was held as to the appropriate sentence. Strickland (D) was sentenced to death. He petitioned for certiorari to the United States Supreme Court, contending that he was denied effective assistance of counsel in violation of the Sixth Amendment. [The casebook excerpt did not state the basis for Strickland's (D) claim.]

ISSUE: Must a court deciding an ineffectiveness of counsel claim at a death sentence hearing judge whether counsel's conduct was reasonable as viewed at the time of the alleged ineffectiveness?

HOLDING AND DECISION: (O'Connor, J.) Yes. A court deciding an ineffectiveness of counsel claim at a death sentence hearing must judge whether counsel's conduct was reasonable as viewed at the time of the alleged ineffectiveness, and the defendant, having shown such ineffectiveness, must demonstrate a reasonable probability that the outcome would have been different but for the mistake. Since a death sentence hearing is an adversarial process not unlike a trial, the standard for a claim of constitutional ineffectiveness at the hearing is like that for trial: the defendant must show that counsel made errors so serious that counsel was not functioning as "counsel." Secondly, the defendant must show that the deficient performance so prejudiced the defense as to deprive the defendant of a fair trial. The proper standard for attorney performance is that of reasonably effective assistance; and what is "reasonable" must be viewed in light of what counsel knew or should have known at the time of trial. Courts should not indulge in hindsight or second-guessing of counsel lightly; it is presumed that counsel fulfilled its duty of loyalty and competence. To hold that courts can at-will scrutinize performance of counsel would encourage proliferation of ineffectiveness challenges. Therefore, only if a court can say that counsel definitely committed errors that should not have been made considering that which it knew or should have known at the time of the errors will counsel be considered ineffective. As to the prejudice requirement, it is not enough to show the mere possibility of prejudice. Such possibility will always exist, and more is required to show constitutional error. Rather, a defendant must show that confidence in the outcome has been undermined. This Court believes that the proper standard is that it be reasonably probable that the ineffectiveness altered the outcome of the proceeding. [The casebook excerpt omitted analysis of the facts of the case to the standard described herein.]

ANALYSIS

Rule 8.6(a) of the ABA standards relating to the Defense Function provides: "If a lawyer, after investigation, is satisfied that another lawyer who served in an earlier phase of the case did not provide effective assistance, he should not hesitate to seek relief for the defendant on that ground." This would seem to provide an invitation for ineffectiveness challenges. However, as the present opinion makes clear, the Court is not disposed toward such challenges.

Quicknotes

CERTIORARI A discretionary writ issued by a superior court to an inferior court in order to review the lower court's decisions; the Supreme Court's writ ordering such review.

INEFFECTIVE ASSISTANCE OF COUNSEL A claim brought by an accused in which it must be determined whether the attorney's rendering of representation was such that the ultimate disposition of the case may not be relied upon as fair.

Padilla v. Kentucky

Individual (P) v. State (D)

559 U.S. 356 (2010).

NATURE OF CASE: Certiorari review of motion for post-conviction relief.

FACT SUMMARY: After pleading guilty to drug crimes, Padilla (P) faces deportation. He appealed arguing ineffective assistance of counsel for failure to advise him of the effect of his plea.

RULE OF LAW

A criminal defense attorney has an obligation to advise his or her client that pleading guilty to a charge may lead to deportation, and an attorney's failure to so advise will provide grounds for a claim of ineffective assistance of counsel.

FACTS: Padilla (P) was charged with drug crimes. His attorney informed him pleading guilty to the charge would not affect his immigration status. After pleading guilty, Padilla (P) faces deportation. Padilla (P) filed a petition for post-conviction relief [which was denied]. The United States Supreme Court granted Padilla's (P) petition for review.

ISSUE: Does a criminal defense attorney have an obligation to advise his or her client that pleading guilty to a charge may lead to deportation, and will an attorney's failure to so advise, provide grounds for a claim of ineffective assistance of counsel?

HOLDING AND DECISION: (Stevens, J.) Yes. A criminal defense attorney has an obligation to advise his or her client that pleading guilty to a charge may lead to deportation, and an attorney's failure to so advise will provide grounds for a claim of ineffective assistance of counsel. To state a claim for ineffective assistance of counsel, a plaintiff must show a counsel's representation fell below the objective standard of reasonableness. The second step is to determine whether the result of the criminal matter would have been different but for the errors of the counsel. Almost all bar associations require defense counsel advise their clients as to the risk of deportation. Moreover, a simple review of the relevant statute in this case would have made Padilla's (P) counsel aware a conviction would lead to deportation. Accordingly, Padilla (P) has stated a claim for ineffective assistance of counsel based on his attorney's incorrect assertions a guilty plea would not affect his immigration status. However, Padilla (P) must still prove the ineffective assistance he received was prejudicial to him. Reversed and remanded.

ANALYSIS

In state courts across the country, for a noncitizen criminal defendant, the ramifications of a guilty plea on his or her immigration status is paramount. The possibility of deportation plays a large role in the plea negotiations between prosecutors and defense counsel. Often, criminal defendants will accept guilty pleas to lesser, misdemeanor charges that will not result in deportation.

Quicknotes

INEFFECTIVE ASSISTANCE OF COUNSEL A claim brought by an accused in which it must be determined whether the attorney's rendering of representation was such that the ultimate disposition of the case may not be relied upon as fair.

Control of Quality: Nonlawyers in the Law Business (and Related Issues)

Quick Reference Rules of Law

PAGE

1. *NAACP v. Button.* A state may not constitutionally prohibit the solicitation of clients by an agent of an individual or organization that retains a lawyer in connection with an action in which it is neither a party nor has a pecuniary interest. — 90

2. *In re Primus.* A state may not prohibit attorneys from mailing letters to potential clients advising them of their legal rights and of the opportunity to receive free legal services. — 92

3. *United Transportation Union v. State Bar of Michigan.* A labor union can assist its members in obtaining low-cost legal services. — 93

NAACP v. Button

Political organization (P) v. State official (D)

371 U.S. 415 (1963).

NATURE OF CASE: Review of order rejecting constitutional challenge to anti-solicitation law.

FACT SUMMARY: Virginia (D) enacted a law prohibiting the solicitation of clients by an agent of an organization or individual that retained a lawyer in connection with an action in which it was neither a party nor had a pecuniary interest.

RULE OF LAW

A state may not constitutionally prohibit the solicitation of clients by an agent of an individual or organization that retains a lawyer in connection with an action in which it is neither a party nor has a pecuniary interest.

FACTS: The Virginia Chapter of the National Association for the Advancement of Colored People (the NAACP) (P) had for years engaged in the activity of locating (soliciting) potential plaintiffs to be litigants in suits aimed at fulfilling the NAACP's (P) political objectives of ending segregation. In response, the state of Virginia (D) enacted an anti-solicitation law prohibiting the agent of an organization or individual from soliciting clients for lawsuits in which the organization or individual paid for the lawyer in connection with an action in which the organization or individual was neither a party nor had a pecuniary interest. Because the attorneys to whom the NAACP (P) would refer potential litigants were usually on the NAACP (P) staff, this effectively prohibited the NAACP's (P) solicitation procedure. The NAACP (P) challenged this as violative of the First Amendment. The state's highest court rejected this contention, and the United States Supreme Court granted certiorari.

ISSUE: May a state constitutionally prohibit the solicitation of clients by an agent of an individual or organization that retains a lawyer in connection with an action in which it is neither a party nor has a pecuniary interest?

HOLDING AND DECISION: (Brennan, J.) No. A state may not constitutionally prohibit the solicitation of clients by an agent of an individual or organization that retains a lawyer in connection with an action in which it is neither a party nor has a pecuniary interest. Solicitation is covered by the First Amendment, since abstract discussion is not the only species of communication protected by the First Amendment; vigorous advocacy is protected by it as well. Litigation is more than a vehicle for resolving private disputes; it is a means for achieving lawful political ends, and in that regard it is political expression. Under the conditions of government, litigation is sometimes the only practicable way an unpopular group can petition for redress of grievances. The First Amendment protects certain forms of group activity, and using litigation to achieve political ends is one such form of activity. That is, association for litigation is a form of political association. Under the statute at issue, a person who advises another that his legal rights have been infringed and refers him to a particular attorney or group of attorneys for assistance has committed a crime, as has the attorney who knowingly renders assistance under such circumstances; the statute thus poses the grave danger of unconstitutionally eliminating any discussion relating to the institution of litigation on behalf of unpopular minorities. Since the use of litigation is a constitutionally protected activity, Virginia (D) must show a compelling reason for its existence. The proffered justification is the state interest in regulating the legal profession and against solicitation and barratry. While these are important objectives, the type of solicitation at issue here differs materially from solicitation of a for-profit nature, which a state may well be able to prohibit. Such is not at issue here. Since a compelling reason for the prohibition has not been shown, it is constitutionally defective. Reversed.

DISSENT: (Harlan, J.) An attorney retained by the NAACP (P) to promote its causes—ordinarily an NAACP (P) staff attorney—does not form a normal attorney-client relationship with his "client." The form of pleading, the relief requested, and the timing of lawsuits are all decided by the NAACP (P), not the attorney, to whom he is essentially beholden. Virginia (D) has an interest in maintaining high professional standards in its legal profession. It has never been seriously disputed that laws against solicitation and barratry are valid, and the law at issue finds its roots therein. The majority distinguishes the statute from other types of regulation of solicitation and barratry by noting that the type of suits the NAACP (P) initiates are not of the for-profit nature. This is a too-facile analysis, since the avoidance of pecuniary gain is not the only relevant factor in determining appropriate standards of lawyer conduct. A lawyer in the type of actions maintained by the NAACP (P) finds himself in a divided allegiance. A state has an interest in preventing attorney conflicts of interest, and this legitimizes the law in question. Moreover, the statute here does not unreasonably impede the assertion of federal rights and is consistent with federal standing rules.

Continued on next page.

▶ ANALYSIS

Ethical Consideration 5-1 of Canon 5 of the ABA Code of Professional Responsibility provides: "The professional judgment of a lawyer should be exercised, within the bounds of the law, solely for the benefit of his client and free of compromising influences and loyalties. Neither his personal interests, the interests of other clients, nor the desires of third persons should be permitted to dilute his loyalty to his client." An attorney retained by an organization which has solicited litigants to further its political ends through litigation will almost certainly have to deal with this consideration at some point, and may at some point face a conflict of interest that will require the attorney's withdrawal.

■□■

Quicknotes

CONFLICT OF INTEREST Refers to ethical problems that arise, or may be anticipated to arise, between an attorney and his client if the interests of the attorney, another client or a third party conflict with those of the present client.

RETAINER Compensation paid in advance for professional services.

■□■

In re Primus

N/A

436 U.S. 412 (1978).

NATURE OF CASE: Review of attorney reprimand.

FACT SUMMARY: The South Carolina Bar reprimanded Primus for forwarding a letter to an individual advising her of certain rights and of the opportunity to receive free legal services.

> ### 🏛 RULE OF LAW
> A state may not prohibit attorneys from mailing letters to potential clients advising them of their legal rights and of the opportunity to receive free legal services.

FACTS: Primus, an attorney, in conjunction with the American Civil Liberties Union (ACLU), forwarded a letter to one Williams, who had been sterilized as part of a state regulatory practice conditioning entitlement to welfare payments on sterilization. The letter advised Williams that she had a potential claim against the doctor who performed the procedure, and that the ACLU had a legal staff that could perform free legal services for her. Williams declined to pursue the matter, but the state bar, under a disciplinary rule prohibiting solicitation by letter, published a letter of reprimand against Primus. The South Carolina Supreme Court affirmed the reprimand, and the United States Supreme Court granted review.

ISSUE: May a state prohibit attorneys from mailing letters to potential clients advising them of their legal rights and of the opportunity to receive free legal services?

HOLDING AND DECISION: (Powell, J.) No. A state may not prohibit attorneys from mailing letters to potential clients advising them of their legal rights and of the opportunity to receive free legal services. When legal services are performed as part of an attempt to further a political agenda, such activities constitute a form of expression protected under the First and Fourteenth Amendments. State abridgements on such activities must be narrowly tailored to serve a compelling interest. Here, there can be little question but that Primus's solicitation was part of an effort to advance a political program; the ACLU is well known for taking political positions, and the fact that it might benefit at some later date because of a regulated lawsuit does not alter this. Consequently, Primus's letter was a form of protected expression. The proffered state interest is the prevention of overreaching and intimidation of potential clients. While a state has a compelling interest in prohibiting this behavior, it has not been shown that a blanket prohibition on solicitation by mail is necessary to achieve this end. Since the state prohibition is not narrowly drawn, it is unconstitutional. Reversed.

▶ ANALYSIS

This case was decided the same day as *Ohralik v. Ohio State Bar Assn.*, 436 U.S. 447 (1978). These two cases appear to show the outer limits of a state's ability to prohibit attorney solicitation. It would seem the cases can be read to permit a state to prohibit completely all attorney in-person solicitation. All other solicitations, if politically motivated, must be reviewed on a case-by-case basis.

■▬■

Quicknotes

COMMERCIAL SPEECH Any speech that proposes a commercial transaction or promotes products or services.

FREEDOM OF ASSOCIATION The right to peaceably assemble.

■▬■

United Transportation Union v. State Bar of Michigan

Railworkers' union (D) v. Michigan state bar (P)

401 U.S. 576 (1971).

NATURE OF CASE: Review of order enjoining a labor union from procuring legal services for its members.

FACT SUMMARY: The Michigan State Bar (P) challenged the United Transportation Union's (D) practice of obtaining low-cost legal services for its members.

🏛 RULE OF LAW
A labor union can assist its members in obtaining low-cost legal services.

FACTS: The United Transportation Union (the Union) (D) instituted a program to assist its members who had causes of action under the Federal Employers' Liability Act. The Union (D) would refer its members to selected attorneys, who had agreed to charge a fee of no more than 25 percent of total recovery. The Michigan State Bar (P) challenged this practice as illegal "solicitation" of lawsuits. A state trial court enjoined the practice, and the Michigan Supreme Court affirmed. The United States Supreme Court granted review.

ISSUE: Can a labor union assist its members in obtaining low-cost legal services?

HOLDING AND DECISION: (Black, J.) Yes. A labor union can assist its members in obtaining low-cost legal services. This Court has already held that the First Amendment permits groups to unite to assert their legal rights as effectively and economically as possible. An organization may also employ attorneys to represent its members. From this it follows that an organization may also refer its members to attorneys. The injunction at issue here not only prohibited the Union (D) from so doing, but also enjoined it from doing various acts incident thereto, such as providing information concerning the availability of legal service and compensating individuals for the time spent providing such information. If an organization is to be permitted to assert its legal rights, the activities enjoined in this particular case must also be permitted. Reversed.

▌ *ANALYSIS*

The case principally relied upon by the Court here was *NAACP v. Button*, 371 U.S. 415 (1963). A difference existed between the situation in *NAACP* and the present case, in that the prior action involved ideologically motivated litigation as opposed to the purely economic interests at issue here. It is not clear whether this distinction was raised, and based on the Court's inclinations as evidenced by the language of the opinion, it is unlikely that it would have altered the holding.

■=■

Quicknotes

FIRST AMENDMENT Prohibits Congress from enacting any law respecting an establishment of religion, prohibiting the free exercise of religion, abridging freedom of speech or the press, the right of peaceful assembly and the right to petition for a redress of grievances.

■=■

CHAPTER 15

Free Speech Rights of Lawyers and Judicial Candidates

Quick Reference Rules of Law

Gentile v. State Bar of Nevada

Criminal defense attorney (D) v. Nevada state bar (P)

501 U.S. 1030 (1991).

NATURE OF CASE: Review of attorney disciplinary order of reprimand.

FACT SUMMARY: Gentile (D), who spoke to the press about a pending prosecution, contended that such speech was constitutionally protected and could only be prohibited when it constituted a clear and present danger to a fair trial.

🏛 RULE OF LAW

(1) A state's rule of conduct is unconstitutionally void for vagueness where it is written in such a way that it does not clearly demarcate the line between permitted and prohibited conduct.

(2) Public utterances by an attorney need not present a clear and present danger to a fair trial to be subject to prohibition.

FACTS: Gentile (D), a Nevada attorney, undertook to represent Sanders, who had been indicted for theft of money and drugs that the police had placed in a safety deposit box as part of a sting operation. For months, the local media issued reports about the investigation into the theft and which speculated whether police officers were responsible, or whether Sanders, as the owner of the vaults in which the safety deposit box had been kept was the culprit. Six months prior to trial (at which Sanders was ultimately acquitted), Gentile (D) held a press conference wherein he made certain charges of a cover-up by local police and prosecutors. His intent in calling the conference was to counter prejudicial publicity that had already been broadcast, as well as to defend Sanders' reputation. Before calling the conference, he carefully studied Nevada Supreme Court Rule 177, which prohibited an attorney from speaking about a pending case if such speech had a "substantial likelihood of materially prejudicing" the outcome of the case, and he decided that given the trial was not for six months, what he had to say would not be prejudicial. The Nevada State Bar (P) subsequently recommended that Gentile (D) be privately reprimanded for violating Rule 177, and the state's Supreme Court affirmed. However, Rule 177(3) provided a safe harbor that permitted an attorney to "state without elaboration . . . the general nature of the . . . defense," and Gentile (D) contended that he believed his press conference was protected by this provision. Gentile (D) petitioned for certiorari, contending, inter alia, that Rule 177 was vague and therefore void, and that, consistent with the First Amendment, only speech showing a clear and present danger of denying a fair trial could be prohibited. The United States Supreme

Court granted the requested certiorari. Justice Kennedy delivered the opinion of the Court with respect to Parts III and VI, concluding that, as interpreted by the Nevada Supreme Court, Rule 177 is void for vagueness. Chief Justice Rehnquist delivered the opinion of the Court with respect to Parts I and II, concluding that the "substantial likelihood of material prejudice" test applied by Nevada and most other States satisfies the First Amendment.

ISSUE:

(1) Is a state's rule of conduct unconstitutionally void for vagueness where it is written in such a way that it does not clearly demarcate the line between permitted and prohibited conduct?

(2) Must public utterances by an attorney present a clear and present danger to a fair trial to be subject to prohibition?

HOLDING AND DECISION: (Kennedy, J.)

(1) Yes. A state's rule of conduct is unconstitutionally void for vagueness where it is written in such a way that it does not clearly demarcate the line between permitted and prohibited conduct. Rule 177 is void for vagueness. Its safe harbor provision, Rule 177(3), misled Gentile (D) into thinking that he could give his press conference without fear of discipline. Given the Rule's grammatical structure and the absence of a clarifying interpretation by the state court, the Rule fails to provide fair notice to those to whom it is directed and is so imprecise that discriminatory enforcement is a real possibility. By necessary operation of the word "notwithstanding," the Rule contemplates that a lawyer describing the "general" nature of the defense without "elaboration" need fear no discipline even if he knows or reasonably should know that his statement will have a substantial likelihood of materially prejudicing an adjudicative proceeding. Both "general" and "elaboration" are classic terms of degree that, in this context, have no settled usage or tradition of interpretation in law, and thus a lawyer has no principle for determining when his remarks pass from the permissible to the forbidden. A review of the press conference—where Gentile (D) made only a brief opening statement and declined to answer reporters' questions seeking more detailed comments—supports his claim that he thought his statements were protected. That he was found in violation of the Rules after studying them and making a conscious effort at compliance shows that Rule 177 creates a trap for the wary as well as the unwary. Reversed on these grounds.

Continued on next page.

[Parts IV and V] Contrary to the majority's decision as to the appropriate standard of review to apply, restrictions on an attorney's speech should not be assessed under a standard that is more deferential to state interests than is the usual rule where speech is concerned where the speech involved is neither commercial nor pertaining to information the attorney could obtain only through the court's discovery process. Here, Gentile's (D) press conference statements fell into neither category that warrants a more deferential standard. Instead, Gentile (D) was disciplined because he proclaimed to the community what he thought to be a misuse of the prosecutorial and police powers; wide-open balancing of interests is not appropriate in such a context. Rule 177, on its face and as applied here, is neither limited to nor even directed at preventing release of information received through court proceedings or special access afforded attorneys, but encompasses all attorney speech. However, even if such a deferential standard is correctly applied to the restrictions set forth in the Rule, the Rule—as interpreted by the Nevada Supreme Court—was invalid under that standard. First, empirical research suggests that in the few instances when jurors have been exposed to extensive and prejudicial publicity, they are able to disregard it and base their verdict upon the evidence presented in court. Second, still less justification exists for a lower standard of scrutiny here, as the speech involved not the prosecutor or police, but a criminal defense attorney. There is no empirical or anecdotal evidence of a need for restrictions on defense publicity. The police, the prosecution, other government officials, and the community at large hold innumerable avenues for the dissemination of information adverse to a criminal defendant, many of which are not within the scope of Rule 177 or any other regulation. By contrast, a defendant cannot speak without fear of incriminating himself and prejudicing his defense, and most criminal defendants have insufficient means to retain a public relations team apart from defense counsel for the sole purpose of countering prosecution statements. These factors underscore the conclusion that blanket rules restricting speech of defense attorneys should not be accepted without careful First Amendment scrutiny. In sum, at least in this case, Rule 177 as applied here represents a limitation of First Amendment freedoms greater than is necessary or essential to the protection of the governmental interest in fair trials, and does not protect against a danger of the necessary gravity, imminence, or likelihood. Because it cannot be said that Gentile's (D) conduct demonstrated any real or specific threat to the legal process, his statements must have the full protection of the First Amendment.

(2) (Rehnquist, C.J.) No. Public utterances by an attorney need not present a clear and present danger to a fair trial to be subject to prohibition. An attorney does not park his free speech rights at the courthouse door.

Nonetheless, the governmental interest in ensuring fair trials exerts sufficient influence on an attorney's role that, to the extent an attorney's speech might tend to have improper influence on a case, that speech may be regulated under a standard less demanding than that of "clear and present danger." Precedent also makes plain that the speech of lawyers representing clients in pending cases may be regulated under a less demanding standard than that established for regulation of the press. The standard employed here, that of "substantial likelihood of material prejudice," has been adopted by a majority of states, and this Court agrees that it represents a proper balancing of an attorney's free speech rights with the state's interest in a fair trial, and hereby adopts it as the appropriate standard in this area.

DISSENT: (Rehnquist, C.J.) [Dissent is to Part III.] Contrary to the majority's conclusion, Rule 177 is not vague. It provided adequate notice to Gentile (D) that his conduct was prohibited. Although the list of conduct likely to cause prejudice was only advisory, the Rule certainly gave notice that the statements made would violate the Rule if they had the intended effect, i.e., of influencing the jury. Moreover, no sensible person could think that Gentile's (D) statements were "general" statements of a claim or defense made "without elaboration." Gentile's (D) strongest arguments are that the statements were made well in advance of trial, and that the statements did not in fact taint the jury panel. However, as the Supreme Court of Nevada pointed out, his statements were not only highly inflammatory, but were timed to have maximum impact, when public interest in the case was at its height immediately after Sanders was indicted. Thus, his remarks were "substantially likely to cause material prejudice" to the proceedings. Also rejected is the argument that the First Amendment requires the State to show actual prejudice to a judicial proceeding before an attorney may be disciplined for extrajudicial statements. Not only is this another way of restating the already-rejected position that the same standard should apply to attorneys that applies to the press, but adopting this stricter standard would permit attorneys to make comments more flagrant than those made by Gentile (D) without fear of disciplinary action if, for wholly independent reasons, they had no effect on the proceedings. For example, an attorney who made prejudicial comments would be insulated from discipline if the government, for reasons unrelated to the comments, decided to dismiss the charges, or if a plea bargain were reached.

CONCURRENCE: (O'Connor, J.) Although a State may regulate speech by lawyers representing clients in pending cases more readily than it may regulate the press, here Gentile (D) seemed to have stayed within Rule 177's

Continued on next page.

safe haven provisions, and the State Bar's (P) view that he did not underscores its vagueness.

▶ ANALYSIS

Attorney freedom-of-speech issues usually arise in the context of advertising, a form of commercial speech. The impact of the First Amendment on commercial speech is somewhat different to that involved here. The analysis used here is not necessarily applicable to advertising cases.

▬▬

Quicknotes

NEVADA SUPREME COURT RULE 177 Prohibits the dissemination of information that an attorney knows or reasonably should know has a substantial likelihood of materially prejudicing an adjudicative proceeding.

In re Holtzman

N/A

N.Y. Ct. App., 78 N.Y.2d 184, 577 N.E.2d 30, *cert. denied*, 502 U.S. 1009 (1991).

NATURE OF CASE: Appeal of admonition for attorney conduct.

FACT SUMMARY: Holtzman (D), admonished for falsely accusing a judge of improper behavior, contended that such an admonition required a finding of constitutional malice.

RULE OF LAW

It is not necessary for an attorney to act with constitutional malice in order for the attorney to be disciplined for issuing false statements.

FACTS: Holtzman (D), the Kings County District Attorney, released a letter to the media alleging that a trial court judge behaved improperly. An investigation revealed that her accusations were false. She was then admonished under attorney disciplinary rules for the false accusations. She appealed the admonition, contending that state bar authorities had to find that she acted with constitutional malice in order to discipline her.

ISSUE: Is it necessary for an attorney to act with constitutional malice in order for the attorney to be disciplined for issuing false statements?

HOLDING AND DECISION: (Per curiam) No. It is not necessary for an attorney to act with constitutional malice in order for the attorney to be disciplined for issuing false statements. Unlike defamation, to which constitutional malice applies, professional responsibility is not an essentially private matter but rather is rendered for the benefit of the public at large. When an attorney makes a false statement, the issue is not whether a reputation has been harmed but rather whether the administration of justice has been hampered. To substitute objective analysis of this question with the subjective standard of constitutional malice would undercut the premise of professional responsibility, which would be against the public interest. Affirmed.

▶ *ANALYSIS*

In the adversarial atmosphere of the courtroom, it is natural that attorneys and judges will lock horns. This sometimes results in public statements by attorneys about judges that are less than flattering. All states have limits on what attorneys can say about judges, limits which attorneys often cross to their regret.

Quicknotes

MALICE The intention to commit an unlawful act without justification or excuse.

NEW YORK CODE OF PROFESSIONAL RESPONSIBILITY DR 1-102(A)(6) A lawyer shall not engage in any other conduct that adversely reflects on his fitness to practice law.

Republican Party of Minnesota v. White

Political party (P) v. State judicial official (D)

536 U.S. 765 (2002).

NATURE OF CASE: Appeal from decision that a state's judiciary, without violating the First Amendment, may prohibit candidates for judicial election in that state from announcing their views on disputed legal or political issues.

FACT SUMMARY: The state's highest court adopted a canon of judicial conduct that prohibited a candidate for judicial office from "announc[ing] his or her views on disputed legal or political issues" (announce clause). While running for associate justice of that court, Wersal (and others) (P) filed suit seeking a declaration that the announce clause violated the First Amendment.

RULE OF LAW
The First Amendment prohibits a state's judiciary from prohibiting candidates for judicial election in that state from announcing their views on disputed legal and political issues.

FACTS: The state's highest court adopted a canon of judicial conduct that prohibited a "candidate for a judicial office" from "announc[ing] his or her views on disputed legal or political issues" (announce clause). Incumbent judges who violated this rule were subject to discipline, including removal, censure, civil penalties, and suspension without pay. Lawyers who ran for judicial office also had to comply with the announce clause. While running for associate justice of the state's highest court, Wersal (and others) (P) filed suit in federal district court seeking a declaration that the announce clause was violative of the First Amendment and an injunction against its enforcement. The district court held that the announce clause was constitutional and granted summary judgment to the state (D). The court of appeals affirmed, and the United States Supreme Court granted certiorari.

ISSUE: Does the First Amendment prohibit a state's judiciary from prohibiting candidates for judicial election in that state from announcing their views on disputed legal and political issues?

HOLDING AND DECISION: (Scalia, J.) Yes. The First Amendment prohibits a state's judiciary from prohibiting candidates for judicial election in that state from announcing their views on disputed legal and political issues. "Announcing views" on an issue covers much more than promising to decide an issue a certain way, and the announce clause prohibits a candidate's mere statements of his current position, even if he doesn't bind himself to maintain that position after election. Although the clause

was construed in the courts below to reach only disputed issues that are likely to come before the candidate if he is elected, this limitation is not much of a limitation because there is almost no legal or political issue that is unlikely to come before a judge of an American court. The record demonstrates that the announce clause prohibits a judicial candidate from stating his views on any specific nonfanciful legal question within the province of the court for which he is running, except in the context of discussing past decisions—and in the latter context as well, if he expresses the view that he is not bound by stare decisis. The state (D) argues that this still leaves plenty of topics for discussion on the campaign trail, such as a candidate's character, education, work habits, etc., and, in fact, the state's (D) judicial board has published a list of preapproved questions that judicial candidates are allowed to answer. The issue then becomes whether these preapproved subjects fulfill the First Amendment's free speech guarantee. The announce clause both prohibits speech based on its content and burdens a category of speech that is at the core of First Amendment freedoms—speech about the qualifications of candidates for public office. The court of appeals concluded, and the parties do not dispute, that the proper test to be applied to determine the constitutionality of such a restriction is strict scrutiny, under which respondents have the burden to prove that the clause is (1) narrowly tailored, to serve (2) a compelling state interest. That court found that the state (D) had established two interests as sufficiently compelling to justify the announce clause: preserving the state judiciary's impartiality and preserving the appearance of that impartiality. Under any definition of "impartiality," the announce-clause fails strict scrutiny. First, it is plain that the clause is not narrowly tailored to serve impartiality (or its appearance) in the traditional sense of the word, i.e., as a lack of bias for or against either party to the proceeding. Indeed, the clause is barely tailored to serve that interest at all, inasmuch as it does not restrict speech for or against particular parties, but rather speech for or against particular issues. If a party loses a case that turns on a legal issue the judge had taken a stand on as a candidate, it is not because of bias against the party, but because the judge is evenhandedly applying the law as he sees it—any party coming before the judge taking a position contrary to the judge's view would lose. Second, although "impartiality" in the sense of a lack of preconception in favor of or against a particular legal view may well be an interest served by the announce clause, pursuing this objective is not a compelling state interest, since it is virtually impossible, and hardly

Continued on next page.

desirable, to find a judge who does not have preconceptions about the law. In fact, the state's constitution positively forbids the selection to courts of judges who are impartial in the sense of having no views on the law because all judges must be learned in the law. Third, the Court need not decide whether achieving "impartiality" (or its appearance) in the sense of openmindedness is a compelling state interest because, as a means of pursuing this interest, the announce clause is so woefully underinclusive that the Court does not believe it was adopted for that purpose. This is demonstrated by the fact that statements made in an election campaign are an infinitesimal portion of the statements judges and judges-to-be make that commit them to a legal position, because they have committed themselves before coming to the bench or while on the bench. Such commitments have been made in prior rulings or in nonadjudicatory settings, such as in classes they conduct, books, and speeches. Thus, a candidate for judicial office may make such a commitment before he announces his candidacy or after he is elected. Justice Stevens asserts in his dissent that statements made in an election campaign pose a special threat to openmindedness because the candidate, when elected judge, will have a particular reluctance to contradict them. While this may be true with regard to campaign promises, promises are not at issue here because they are regulated separately. Also, with regard to nonpromissory commitments to a certain position, it is not self-evident that judges will find these more binding on them than a carefully considered holding. The state (D) has not carried the burden imposed by strict scrutiny of establishing that statements made during an election campaign are uniquely destructive of openmindedness. Justice Stevens is wrong in his broad assertion that to the extent statements on legal issues seek to enhance a candidate's popularity they evidence a lack of fitness for office. Such statements are made in all confirmation hearings, and thus Justice Stevens must think the entire federal bench is unfit. Moreover, the notion that the special context of electioneering justifies an abridgment of the right to speak out on disputed issues sets First Amendment jurisprudence on its head. We have never allowed the government to prohibit candidates from communicating relevant information to voters during an election, but Justice Ginsburg would do so. She contends that the announce clause must be constitutional because due process would be denied if an elected judge sat in a case involving an issue on which he had previously announced his view. She reaches this conclusion because, she says, such a judge would have a "direct, personal, substantial, and pecuniary interest" in ruling consistently with his previously announced view, in order to reduce the risk that he will be "voted off the bench and thereby lose his salary and emoluments," but elected judges—regardless of whether they have announced any views beforehand—always face the pressure of an electorate who might disagree with their rulings and therefore vote them off the bench. If it violates due process for a judge to sit in a case in which ruling one way rather than another

increases his prospects for reelection, then by Justice Ginsburg's logic, the practice of electing judges is itself a violation of due process. Finally, although a universal and long-established tradition of prohibiting certain conduct creates a strong presumption the prohibition is constitutional, the practice of prohibiting speech by judicial candidates is neither ancient nor universal. The Court knows of no such prohibitions throughout the 19th and the first quarter of the 20th century, and they are still not universally adopted. This does not compare well with the traditions deemed worthy of attention. There is an obvious tension between the state's constitution, which requires judicial elections, and the announce clause, which places most subjects of interest to the voters off limits. The First Amendment does not permit the state (D) to leave the principle of elections in place while preventing candidates from discussing what the elections are about. Reversed.

CONCURRENCE: (O'Connor, J.) The very practice of electing judges undermines the state's interest in an impartial judiciary. If judges are subject to regular elections they are likely to feel that they have at least some personal stake in the outcome of every publicized case. Even if judges were able to suppress their awareness of the potential electoral consequences of their decisions and refrain from acting on it, the public's confidence in the judiciary could be undermined simply by the possibility that judges would be unable to do so. Moreover, contested elections generally entail campaigning, which can require substantial funds. Even if judges were able to refrain from favoring donors, the mere possibility that judges' decisions may be motivated by the desire to repay campaign contributors is likely to undermine the public's confidence in the judiciary.

CONCURRENCE: (Kennedy, J.) Content-based speech restrictions that do not fall within any traditional exception should be invalidated without inquiry into narrow tailoring or compelling government interests. The speech at issue here does not come within any of the exceptions to the First Amendment recognized by the Court. The state (D) may not censor what the people hear as they undertake to decide for themselves which candidate is most likely to be an exemplary judicial officer. Deciding the relevance of candidate speech is the right of the voters, not the state. Accordingly, the announce clause contradicts the principle that unabridged speech is the cornerstone of political freedom.

DISSENT: (Stevens, J.) The Court's disposition rests on two seriously flawed premises: (1) an inaccurate appraisal of the importance of judicial independence and impartiality, and (2) an assumption that judicial candidates should have the same freedom to express themselves on matters of current public importance as do all other elected officials. There is a critical difference between the work of

Continued on next page.

the judge and the work of other public officials. In a democracy, issues of policy are properly decided by majority vote, and it is the business of legislators and executives to be popular. By contrast, in litigation, issues of law or fact should not be determined by popular vote, and judges must be indifferent to unpopularity. Any judge who faces reelection, however, may believe that he retains his office only so long as his decisions are popular. Nevertheless, the elected judge, like the lifetime appointee, does not serve a constituency while holding that office. Instead, the judge has a duty to uphold the law and to follow the dictates of the Constitution, as well as to make judgment on the merits—not as a mandate from the voters.

DISSENT: (Ginsburg, J.) Elections for political offices, in which the First Amendment holds full sway, must be distinguished from elections designed to select those whose office it is to administer justice without respect to persons. The state's (D) choice to elect its judges does not preclude the state (D) from installing an election process geared to the judicial office. As agents of the people, legislative and executive officials serve in representative capacities, and therefore, candidates for these representative offices must be left free to inform the electorate of their positions on specific issues. Judges, however, are not representatives of particular persons, communities, or parties; they serve no faction or constituency. They must strive to do what is legally right, even in the face of unpopularity. In addition, the majority ignores a crucial limiting construction placed on the announce clause by the courts below. The provision does not bar a candidate from generally stating views on legal questions; it only prevents her from publicly making known how she would decide disputed issues. That limitation places beyond the scope of the announce clause a wide range of comments that may be highly informative to voters, including statements of historical fact; qualified statements; and statements framed at a sufficient level of generality. The announce clause is thus narrower, and campaigns conducted under that provision more robust, than the majority's construction of the clause acknowledges. Judicial candidates may not only convey general information about themselves, but they may describe their conception of the role of a judge and their views on a wide range of subjects of interest to the voters. Further, they may discuss, criticize, or defend past decisions of interest to voters. What they may not do is remove themselves from the constraints characteristic of the judicial office and declare how they would decide an issue, without regard to the particular context in which it is presented. Properly construed, the announce clause prohibits only a discrete subcategory of the statements the majority's misinterpretation encompasses. Moreover, the majority ignores the significance of the announce clause to the state's (D) judicial election system, and its interdependence with the state's (D) rule prohibiting candidates from making pledges or promises of conduct in office other than the faithful and impartial performance of the duties of the office. The pledge or promise rule promotes the public faith in the judiciary by attempting to eliminate the perception that a judge's ruling is merely a quid pro quo for being elected on a campaign promise. The state's (D) interest in the pledges or promises clause is thus significant, and its constitutionality supported. The announce clause is equally important to achieving these constitutional ends, since without it, the pledges or promises clause would be weak. That is because without the announce clause, the pledges and promises clause can be easily circumvented by a candidate who does not promise anything, but merely announces his or her position on a given issue. Both the promise and the statement contemplate a quid pro quo between the candidate and the voters, and, contrary to the majority's belief, the nonpromissory statement does nothing to avert the dangers inherent in the promissory statement. The announce clause prevents this circumvention of the pledges or promises clause, and, therefore is an indispensable—and constitutional—part of the state's (D) effort to maintain a healthy judiciary.

▶ ANALYSIS

This decision presents the difficult issue of whether the restrictions on certain statements made by candidates for judicial office are impermissible content-based restrictions, or permissible content-based restrictions that survive strict scrutiny based on the government's strong interest in preserving judicial independence and impartiality (and the appearance thereof). Hence, the majority focuses on the content of the speech being regulated, whereas the dissent focuses on the government interest. In 2007, the ABA changed its Code of Judicial Conduct to satisfy the decision in this case by eliminating the announce clause and providing an expanded pledges or promises clause.

Quicknotes

CERTIORARI A discretionary writ issued by a superior court to an inferior court in order to review the lower court's decisions; the Supreme Court's writ ordering such review.

FIRST AMENDMENT Prohibits Congress from enacting any law respecting an establishment of religion, prohibiting the free exercise of religion, abridging freedom of speech or the press, the right of peaceful assembly and the right to petition for a redress of grievances.

INJUNCTION A court order requiring a person to do, or prohibiting that person from doing, a specific act.

STARE DECISIS Doctrine whereby courts follow legal precedent unless there is good cause for departure.

Marketing Legal Services

Quick Reference Rules of Law

Ohralik v. Ohio State Bar Assn.

Attorney (D) v. Ohio state bar (P)

436 U.S. 447 (1978).

NATURE OF CASE: Review of order suspending attorney from practice.

FACT SUMMARY: Ohralik (D) solicited two young women who had been in a car accident, visiting one while she was in traction in the hospital.

RULE OF LAW

A state may constitutionally discipline a lawyer for soliciting clients in person, for pecuniary gain, under circumstances likely to pose dangers that the state has a right to prevent.

FACTS: Attorney Ohralik (D), upon learning about an auto accident involving an eighteen-year-old woman, twice visited her in the hospital, whereupon she orally agreed to allow him to represent her. She later sought to renege on the agreement. He also solicited as a client the woman's passenger. The Ohio State Bar (P) instituted disciplinary proceedings, alleging that Ohralik (D) had violated disciplinary rules barring in-person solicitation of clients. Ohralik (D) was indefinitely suspended. The United States Supreme Court granted review.

ISSUE: May a state constitutionally discipline a lawyer for soliciting clients in person?

HOLDING AND DECISION: (Powell, J.) Yes. A state may constitutionally discipline a lawyer for soliciting clients in person, for pecuniary gain, under circumstances likely to pose dangers that the state has a right to prevent. A state has a strong interest in preventing the perceived harms of attorney solicitation, these being assertion of fraudulent claims, debasement of the legal profession, and potential harm to the client by overreaching, overcharging, underrepresentation, and misrepresentation. The potential for coercion of the prospective client is particularly strong in a face-to-face solicitation, as the attorney, who is trained in persuasion, holds a great advantage over the client, who is at best unfamiliar with the law and may be in a particularly vulnerable situation due to whatever misfortune it was that led the attorney to seek him out. For these reasons, a prophylactic rule prohibiting solicitation serves sufficient state interests so as to pass First Amendment scrutiny. Affirmed.

ANALYSIS

At one time, states imposed a near categorical ban on much of the businesslike aspects of law, such as advertising and solicitation. Many of these prohibitions have been lifted after the United States Supreme Court began applying the First Amendment to attorney advertising. Solicitation is the one area that has not changed in this regard.

Quicknotes

COMMERCIAL SPEECH Any speech that proposes a commercial transaction, or promotes products or services.

PROHIBITION AGAINST IN-PERSON SOLICITATION Ethical limits placed on attorneys when seeking to enter into a client relationship, preventing attorney from engaging in coercive or improper behavior when contacting potential clients directly.

Zauderer v. Office of Disciplinary Counsel

Attorney (D) v. Ohio state bar (P)

471 U.S. 626 (1985).

NATURE OF CASE: Appeal from state's highest court decision ordering public reprimand of an attorney based on the attorney's advertisements.

FACT SUMMARY: Attorney Zauderer (D) placed in numerous newspapers an advertisement targeting as potential clients women who had used the Dalkon Shield Intrauterine Device, which was known to cause numerous health problems. The state's Office of Disciplinary Counsel (Office) (P) disciplined him on several grounds for doing so. Zauderer (D) contended that the state could not constitutionally restrict his truthful commercial speech or require that he disclose that clients could be liable for litigation costs.

🏛 **RULE OF LAW**
(1) A state may not prohibit a truthful, nonfraudulent legal service advertisement that does not concern unlawful activities merely because the advertisement contains information or advice regarding a specific legal problem.
(2) Illustrations in legal service advertisements are protected by the First Amendment from regulation where the illustrations are accurate and non-deceptive.
(3) States may constitutionally require that legal service advertisements fully disclose the terms of the type of engagement advertised.

FACTS: Attorney Zauderer (D) placed in 36 newspapers an advertisement identifying the "Dalkon Shield" (IUD) and inviting women who had used the device to contact his office about their legal rights. The ad informed the reader that the device had been found to cause various physical problems and that Zauderer's (D) office was handling a number of cases involving the Shield. The ad also informed the reader that cases were handled on a contingency fee basis, but failed to notify the reader that clients could be liable for legal costs (as opposed to fees) regardless of the success of their claim. The state Office of Disciplinary Counsel (Office) (P) filed a disciplinary action against Zauderer (D), contending that he had violated several state rules against solicitation. These regulations prohibited soliciting legal business through advertisements containing advice and information regarding specific legal problems; placed restrictions on the use of illustrations in advertising by lawyers; and required certain disclosures relating to the terms of contingent fees and litigation costs. The state's highest court upheld the Office's (P) imposition of disci-

pline, ordering that Zauderer (D) be publicly reprimanded, and the United States Supreme Court granted certiorari.

ISSUE:
(1) May a state prohibit a truthful, nonfraudulent legal service advertisement that does not concern unlawful activities merely because the advertisement contains information or advice regarding a specific legal problem?
(2) Are illustrations in legal service advertisements protected by the First Amendment from regulation where the illustrations are accurate and non-deceptive?
(3) May states constitutionally require that legal service advertisements fully disclose the terms of the type of engagement advertised?

HOLDING AND DECISION: (White, J.)
(1) No. A state may not prohibit a truthful, nonfraudulent legal service advertisement that does not concern unlawful activities merely because the advertisement contains information or advice regarding a specific legal problem. This Court has held that government has an interest in prohibiting advertisement that is false, deceptive or misleading, or that concerns unlawful activities. However, when these interests are not implicated, the First Amendment protects commercial speech. Here, the Office (P) contended that Zauderer's (D) advertisement ran afoul of antisolicitation rules. However, it is not clear how the advertisement in question violated these rules. There is no allegation that the ad is false or misleading; in fact, it is not disputed that it is quite accurate. An advertisement such as that at issue here carries none of the potentialities for coercion, overreaching, or intimidation that led this Court to approve of categorical bans on in-person solicitation. Also, there is no evidence that it will "stir up litigation." It is not stirring up litigation to notify people that they may have rights, and litigation undertaken to vindicate rights or redress injuries in good faith is not an evil. Finally, the Office's (P) premise, that it is intrinsically difficult to distinguish advertisements containing legal advice that is false or deceptive from those that are truthful and helpful, is unfounded. In essence, there is no substantial governmental interest that is advanced by a blanket ban on advertisements of this type, so such a ban is unconstitutional. Reversed as to this issue.
(2) Yes. Illustrations in legal service advertisements are protected by the First Amendment from regulation where the illustrations are accurate and non-deceptive. The analysis regarding the illustration of the Dalkon Shield

Continued on next page.

in Zauderer's (D) advertisement is similar to the analysis used to determine whether the government had a substantial interest in regulating the text of the ad. Provided the illustration is non-deceptive, accurate, and unlikely to confuse the reader, it is protected by the First Amendment notwithstanding that some readers might find it offensive or embarrassing. Also rejected is the Office's (P) argument that the use of illustrations in advertising by attorneys creates unacceptable risks that the public will be misled, manipulated, or confused; the Office (P) has failed to present convincing evidence that identifying deceptive or manipulative uses of visual media in advertising is so intrinsically burdensome that the state is entitled to forgo that task in favor of the more convenient but far more restrictive alternative of a blanket ban on the use of illustrations. Reversed as to this issue.

(3) Yes. States may constitutionally require that legal service advertisements fully disclose the terms of the type of engagement advertised. The analysis applied to the text and illustration in Zauderer's (D) ad is inapplicable to the requirement that he disclose the terms of his engagement. That is because, constitutionally speaking, there is a significant difference between outright bans on speech and requiring truthful disclosures. Because the extension of First Amendment protection to commercial speech is justified principally by the value to consumers of the information such speech provides, Zauderer's (D) constitutionally protected interest in not providing any particular factual information in his advertising is minimal. An advertiser's rights are adequately protected as long as disclosure requirements are reasonably related to the state's interest in preventing deception of consumers. The Office's (P) position that it is deceptive to employ advertising that refers to contingent-fee arrangements without mentioning the client's liability for costs is reasonable enough to support the disclosure requirement. Affirmed as to this issue.

DISSENT: (O'Connor, J.) [Justice O'Connor's dissent addressed that portion of the majority's opinion that dealt with the issue of whether a state may prohibit a truthful, nonfraudulent legal service advertisement that does not concern unlawful activities merely because the advertisement contains information or advice regarding a specific legal problem.] The use of unsolicited legal advice to entice clients poses enough of a risk of overreaching and undue influence to warrant the state's rule. First, because professional services are complex, there is a greater possibility of creating confusion and deception. Second, the attorney's self-interest in obtaining business may color the advice given, so that the public will potentially receive advice that is incomplete and/or self-serving. Accordingly, the state has a substantial interest in regulating such speech, and doing so will not reduce the avenues attorneys have for informing the public of their legal rights.

▶ ANALYSIS

Legal advertising is commercial speech. Commercial speech enjoys a more limited protection under the First Amendment than most other types of speech. In most situations, the government must show a "compelling" interest to restrict speech. In commercial speech, the government must show a less burdensome "substantial" interest. Even under this standard, most cases involving attorney advertising in the last two decades have gone against the government.

━■━

Quicknotes

COMMERCIAL SPEECH Any speech that proposes a commercial transaction, or promotes products or services.

━■━

Shapero v. Kentucky Bar Assn.

Kentucky attorney (P) v. State bar association (D)

486 U.S. 466 (1988).

NATURE OF CASE: Review of order upholding the state bar disciplinary rule.

FACT SUMMARY: The Kentucky Bar Association (D) promulgated a disciplinary rule prohibiting the mailing of advertisements for particular legal services.

RULE OF LAW
A state may not prohibit the mailing of advertisements to a target audience believed to be in need of particular legal services.

FACTS: Shapero (P), a Kentucky attorney, applied to the Attorneys Advertising Commission of the Kentucky State Bar (D) for approval of an advertisement he wished to circulate. The advertisement would be sent to those individuals who, according to public records, were facing imminent foreclosure. The ad apprised the recipients that avenues for forestalling foreclosure existed and recommended that the addressee call Shapero's (P) office for a free consultation about their rights in this matter. While not finding the advertisement false or misleading, the Commission (D) found it to conflict with Kentucky Supreme Court Rule 3.135(5)(b)(i), which forbade direct mailing concerning a specific legal matter to one believed to require assistance as to that matter. The State Bar Ethics Committee, on appeal, agreed that the rule precluded the advertisement Shapero (P) wished to make but urged the Supreme Court of Kentucky to amend the rule. It modified the rule, but not so much as to legitimize Shapero's (P) letter. Shapero (P) brought an action seeking to have the rule declared unconstitutional. The United States Court of Appeals upheld the rule, and the United States Supreme Court granted certiorari.

ISSUE: May a state prohibit the mailing of advertisements to a target audience believed to be in need of particular legal services?

HOLDING AND DECISION: (Brennan, J.) No. A state may not prohibit the mailing of advertisements to a target audience believed to be in need of particular legal services. This Court has previously held that the First Amendment protects from state prohibition advertising that is neither false nor misleading. On the other hand, the Court has sanctioned the proscription of in-person solicitation. The factors that led this Court to conclude that solicitation could be banned were primarily the inherently coercive nature of in-person solicitation and the lack of tangible evidence, after the fact, of whether the soliciting attorney in fact overreached during the solicitation. While a direct-mail advertisement is to some extent more coercive than a general, nontargeted advertisement, the recipient in no way can be placed under the same sort of pressures that he could be in a face-to-face situation. Further, unlike in the solicitation situation, the letter itself serves as evidence of whether the advertisement is false or misleading. Since the policy reasons for prohibiting face-to-face solicitation are not present here, the speech in question is protected under the First Amendment. Reversed.

CONCURRENCE AND DISSENT: (White, J.) Any discussion as to whether the advertisement was in fact false or misleading is a matter for state court determination.

DISSENT: (O'Connor, J.) The decision today is consistent with the earlier *Zauderer v. Ohio*, 471 U.S. 626 (1985), but that case was decided upon erroneous grounds. That case improperly applied the usual test that commercial speech is constitutionally protected if it concerns lawful activity and is neither false nor misleading. With respect to advertisements by regulated professions, the states should be free to regulate if the possibility of misleading advertisements exists. The type of advertisements at issue here, certainly contain such possibility.

ANALYSIS

A general rule of thumb can be gleaned from the Court's triumvirate of decisions, *Zauderer, Ohralik v. Ohio State Bar*, 436 U.S. 447 (1978), and the present action. It would seem that outright solicitation, face-to-face, can be categorically banned. An advertisement, even one to a target audience and containing illustrations, may be permitted. However, it must not be misleading and must disclose all or most information necessary for a would-be client to make up his or her mind about using the lawyer's services.

■=■

Quicknotes

COMMERCIAL SPEECH Any speech that proposes a commercial transaction, or promotes products or services.

OVERBREADTH DOCTRINE (Former Rule 7-3 of the Model Rules) Mail solicitation that targets persons known to need legal services is prohibited if a significant motive for the lawyer's doing so is the lawyer's pecuniary gain.

■=■

Glossary

Common Latin Words and Phrases Encountered in the Law

A FORTIORI: Because one fact exists or has been proven, therefore a second fact that is related to the first fact must also exist.

A PRIORI: From the cause to the effect. A term of logic used to denote that when one generally accepted truth is shown to be a cause, another particular effect must necessarily follow.

AB INITIO: From the beginning; a condition which has existed throughout, as in a marriage which was void ab initio.

ACTUS REUS: The wrongful act; in criminal law, such action sufficient to trigger criminal liability.

AD VALOREM: According to value; an ad valorem tax is imposed upon an item located within the taxing jurisdiction calculated by the value of such item.

AMICUS CURIAE: Friend of the court. Its most common usage takes the form of an amicus curiae brief, filed by a person who is not a party to an action but is nonetheless allowed to offer an argument supporting his legal interests.

ARGUENDO: In arguing. A statement, possibly hypothetical, made for the purpose of argument, is one made arguendo.

BILL QUIA TIMET: A bill to quiet title (establish ownership) to real property.

BONA FIDE: True, honest, or genuine. May refer to a person's legal position based on good faith or lacking notice of fraud (such as a bona fide purchaser for value) or to the authenticity of a particular document (such as a bona fide last will and testament).

CAUSA MORTIS: With approaching death in mind. A gift causa mortis is a gift given by a party who feels certain that death is imminent.

CAVEAT EMPTOR: Let the buyer beware. This maxim is reflected in the rule of law that a buyer purchases at his own risk because it is his responsibility to examine, judge, test, and otherwise inspect what he is buying.

CERTIORARI: A writ of review. Petitions for review of a case by the United States Supreme Court are most often done by means of a writ of certiorari.

CONTRA: On the other hand. Opposite. Contrary to.

CORAM NOBIS: Before us; writs of error directed to the court that originally rendered the judgment.

CORAM VOBIS: Before you; writs of error directed by an appellate court to a lower court to correct a factual error.

CORPUS DELICTI: The body of the crime; the requisite elements of a crime amounting to objective proof that a crime has been committed.

CUM TESTAMENTO ANNEXO, ADMINISTRATOR (ADMINISTRATOR C.T.A.): With will annexed; an administrator c.t.a. settles an estate pursuant to a will in which he is not appointed.

DE BONIS NON, ADMINISTRATOR (ADMINISTRATOR D.B.N.): Of goods not administered; an administrator d.b.n. settles a partially settled estate.

DE FACTO: In fact; in reality; actually. Existing in fact but not officially approved or engendered.

DE JURE: By right; lawful. Describes a condition that is legitimate "as a matter of law," in contrast to the term "de facto," which connotes something existing in fact but not legally sanctioned or authorized. For example, de facto segregation refers to segregation brought about by housing patterns, etc., whereas de jure segregation refers to segregation created by law.

DE MINIMIS: Of minimal importance; insignificant; a trifle; not worth bothering about.

DE NOVO: Anew; a second time; afresh. A trial de novo is a new trial held at the appellate level as if the case originated there and the trial at a lower level had not taken place.

DICTA: Generally used as an abbreviated form of obiter dicta, a term describing those portions of a judicial opinion incidental or not necessary to resolution of the specific question before the court. Such nonessential statements and remarks are not considered to be binding precedent.

DUCES TECUM: Refers to a particular type of writ or subpoena requesting a party or organization to produce certain documents in their possession.

EN BANC: Full bench. Where a court sits with all justices present rather than the usual quorum.

EX PARTE: For one side or one party only. An ex parte proceeding is one undertaken for the benefit of only one party, without notice to, or an appearance by, an adverse party.

EX POST FACTO: After the fact. An ex post facto law is a law that retroactively changes the consequences of a prior act.

EX REL.: Abbreviated form of the term "ex relatione," meaning upon relation or information. When the state brings an action in which it has no interest against an individual at the instigation of one who has a private interest in the matter.

FORUM NON CONVENIENS: Inconvenient forum. Although a court may have jurisdiction over the case, the action should be tried in a more conveniently located court, one to which parties and witnesses may more easily travel, for example.

GUARDIAN AD LITEM: A guardian of an infant as to litigation, appointed to represent the infant and pursue his/her rights.

HABEAS CORPUS: You have the body. The modern writ of habeas corpus is a writ directing that a person (body) being detained (such as a prisoner) be brought before the court so that the legality of his detention can be judicially ascertained.

IN CAMERA: In private, in chambers. When a hearing is held before a judge in his chambers or when all spectators are excluded from the courtroom.

IN FORMA PAUPERIS: In the manner of a pauper. A party who proceeds in forma pauperis because of his poverty is one who is allowed to bring suit without liability for costs.

INFRA: Below, under. A word referring the reader to a later part of a book. (The opposite of supra.)

IN LOCO PARENTIS: In the place of a parent.

IN PARI DELICTO: Equally wrong; a court of equity will not grant requested relief to an applicant who is in pari delicto, or as much at fault in the transactions giving rise to the controversy as is the opponent of the applicant.

IN PARI MATERIA: On like subject matter or upon the same matter. Statutes relating to the same person or things are said to be in pari materia. It is a general rule of statutory construction that such statutes should be construed together, i.e., looked at as if they together constituted one law.

IN PERSONAM: Against the person. Jurisdiction over the person of an individual.

IN RE: In the matter of. Used to designate a proceeding involving an estate or other property.

IN REM: A term that signifies an action against the res, or thing. An action in rem is basically one that is taken directly against property, as distinguished from an action in personam, i.e., against the person.

INTER ALIA: Among other things. Used to show that the whole of a statement, pleading, list, statute, etc., has not been set forth in its entirety.

INTER PARTES: Between the parties. May refer to contracts, conveyances or other transactions having legal significance.

INTER VIVOS: Between the living. An inter vivos gift is a gift made by a living grantor, as distinguished from bequests contained in a will, which pass upon the death of the testator.

IPSO FACTO: By the mere fact itself.

JUS: Law or the entire body of law.

LEX LOCI: The law of the place; the notion that the rights of parties to a legal proceeding are governed by the law of the place where those rights arose.

MALUM IN SE: Evil or wrong in and of itself; inherently wrong. This term describes an act that is wrong by its very nature, as opposed to one which would not be wrong but for the fact that there is a specific legal prohibition against it (malum prohibitum).

MALUM PROHIBITUM: Wrong because prohibited, but not inherently evil. Used to describe something that is wrong because it is expressly forbidden by law but that is not in and of itself evil, e.g., speeding.

MANDAMUS: We command. A writ directing an official to take a certain action.

MENS REA: A guilty mind; a criminal intent. A term used to signify the mental state that accompanies a crime or other prohibited act. Some crimes require only a general mens rea (general intent to do the prohibited act), but others, like assault with intent to murder, require the existence of a specific mens rea.

MODUS OPERANDI: Method of operating; generally refers to the manner or style of a criminal in committing crimes, admissible in appropriate cases as evidence of the identity of a defendant.

NEXUS: A connection to.

NISI PRIUS: A court of first impression. A nisi prius court is one where issues of fact are tried before a judge or jury.

N.O.V. (NON OBSTANTE VEREDICTO): Notwithstanding the verdict. A judgment n.o.v. is a judgment given in favor of one party despite the fact that a verdict was returned in favor of the other party, the justification being that the verdict either had no reasonable support in fact or was contrary to law.

NUNC PRO TUNC: Now for then. This phrase refers to actions that may be taken and will then have full retroactive effect.

PENDENTE LITE: Pending the suit; pending litigation under way.

PER CAPITA: By head; beneficiaries of an estate, if they take in equal shares, take per capita.

PER CURIAM: By the court; signifies an opinion ostensibly written "by the whole court" and with no identified author.

PER SE: By itself, in itself; inherently.

PER STIRPES: By representation. Used primarily in the law of wills to describe the method of distribution where a person, generally because of death, is unable to take that which is left to him by the will of another, and therefore his heirs divide such property between them rather than take under the will individually.

PRIMA FACIE: On its face, at first sight. A prima facie case is one that is sufficient on its face, meaning that the evidence supporting it is adequate to establish the case until contradicted or overcome by other evidence.

PRO TANTO: For so much; as far as it goes. Often used in eminent domain cases when a property owner receives partial payment for his land without prejudice to his right to bring suit for the full amount he claims his land to be worth.

QUANTUM MERUIT: As much as he deserves. Refers to recovery based on the doctrine of unjust enrichment in those cases in which a party has rendered valuable services or furnished materials that were accepted and enjoyed by another under circumstances that would reasonably notify the recipient that the rendering party expected to be paid. In essence, the law implies a contract to pay the reasonable value of the services or materials furnished.

QUASI: Almost like; as if; nearly. This term is essentially used to signify that one subject or thing is almost analogous to another but that material differences between them do exist. For example, a quasi-criminal proceeding is one that is not strictly criminal but shares enough of the same characteristics to require some of the same safeguards (e.g., procedural due process must be followed in a parole hearing).

QUID PRO QUO: Something for something. In contract law, the consideration, something of value, passed between the parties to render the contract binding.

RES GESTAE: Things done; in evidence law, this principle justifies the admission of a statement that would otherwise be hearsay when it is made so closely to the event in question as to be said to be a part of it, or with such spontaneity as not to have the possibility of falsehood.

RES IPSA LOQUITUR: The thing speaks for itself. This doctrine gives rise to a rebuttable presumption of negligence when the instrumentality causing the injury was within the exclusive control of the defendant, and the injury was one that does not normally occur unless a person has been negligent.

RES JUDICATA: A matter adjudged. Doctrine which provides that once a court of competent jurisdiction has rendered a final judgment or decree on the merits, that judgment or decree is conclusive upon the parties to the case and prevents them from engaging in any other litigation on the points and issues determined therein.

RESPONDEAT SUPERIOR: Let the master reply. This doctrine holds the master liable for the wrongful acts of his servant (or the principal for his agent) in those cases in which the servant (or agent) was acting within the scope of his authority at the time of the injury.

STARE DECISIS: To stand by or adhere to that which has been decided. The common law doctrine of stare decisis attempts to give security and certainty to the law by following the policy that once a principle of law as applicable to a certain set of facts has been set forth in a decision, it forms a precedent which will subsequently be followed, even though a different decision might be made were it the first time the question had arisen. Of course, stare decisis is not an inviolable principle and is departed from in instances where there is good cause (e.g., considerations of public policy led the Supreme Court to disregard prior decisions sanctioning segregation).

SUPRA: Above. A word referring a reader to an earlier part of a book.

ULTRA VIRES: Beyond the power. This phrase is most commonly used to refer to actions taken by a corporation that are beyond the power or legal authority of the corporation.

Addendum of French Derivatives

IN PAIS: Not pursuant to legal proceedings.

CHATTEL: Tangible personal property.

CY PRES: Doctrine permitting courts to apply trust funds to purposes not expressed in the trust but necessary to carry out the settlor's intent.

PER AUTRE VIE: For another's life; during another's life. In property law, an estate may be granted that will terminate upon the death of someone other than the grantee.

PROFIT A PRENDRE: A license to remove minerals or other produce from land.

VOIR DIRE: Process of questioning jurors as to their predispositions about the case or parties to a proceeding in order to identify those jurors displaying bias or prejudice.